DIVINE HAYFIELDS

ALISON TRIMPER

Published in Australia by Sid Harta Books & Print Pty Ltd,
ABN: 34632585293
23 Stirling Crescent, Glen Waverley, Victoria 3150 Australia
Telephone: +61 3 9560 9920, Facsimile: +61 3 9545 1742
E-mail: author@sidharta.com.au

First published in Australia 2023
This edition published 2023
Copyright © Alison Trimper 2023

Cover design, typesetting: WorkingType (www.workingtype.com.au)

Disclaimer: *Divine Hayfields* is a work of fiction. Characters, their names,
their businesses and the events and incidents involving them are the products
of the author's imagination. Any resemblance to actual persons, living or dead,
or actual events is purely coincidental. While some urban centres mentioned
in the book are real, the village of Wheeler and the properties described are
wholly imaginary.

Alison Trimper
Divine Hayfields
ISBN: 978-1-922958-16-7

About the Author

Alison Trimper has enjoyed a lifelong fascination with words, writing short stories, compiling family anecdotes and writing stories for children. Divine Hayfields is her first foray into the realm of published work. She gathered her understanding of rural life growing up on the family farm near Glen Innes. She and her husband farmed tea trees on the mid-north coast of New South Wales. Alison then became a mature-aged student and completed her education degree, following up with a Masters in Special Education. She greatly enjoyed her years teaching and consistently reminded her students that words, when correctly used, can paint pictures just as detailed and evocative as artists' mediums.

Alison is now retired and lives with her husband on the outskirts of Toowoomba. Her three adult sons and their families are frequent visitors. Alison enjoys cooking for large family gatherings and the leisurely conversation-filled meals that follow. She also enjoys bushwalking and watercolour painting.

Dedication

*My thanks forever to Bob for believing
I could write this book.*

Acknowledgements

During the writing of this book, I spoke to many people about details and ideas. I asked odd questions out of the blue. I would like to thank the many friends, acquaintances and professional people who cheerfully engaged with my questions and, without realising, helped me clarify my thoughts.

My thanks also go to my editor, who patiently dealt with my complete inexperience in the publishing field.

CHAPTER ONE

Felicity Hathaway, forty-six years old, short on stature, large on personality, perched on a stool at her kitchen bench. She meditatively sipped her wine and let her mind drift. She wondered what Gordon was up to in Perth. *Truth be told,* she thought, *his sister's finances were just a cover allowing him to chase himself up a little romance.* She pursued that thought, realising that she wasn't particularly upset to consider it.

Let him have his little secret affair, she thought. *He's not the only one of us with a secret and I've had mine a lot longer than him. We're just about done as a couple really,* she mused. *I can hold my own without him, I'm a successful woman in my own right, he's just an arm decoration. The kids are grown and independent.*

She recognised that she was becoming increasingly frustrated by her constant clashes with Gordon over how her horse stud was to be run. She had another sip, allowing the wine to run slowly down her throat, savouring the sharp flavour. She drifted into a gentle daydream about what direction she would take with the stud, without her husband countermanding her orders and trying to rein in her enthusiasm.

She gave a sharp sigh. *It's my money,* she thought, *my stud, he brought nothing to this deal except his university degree and his big ideas about how to use my money.*

Felicity drained the glass and walked briskly from the kitchen to her bedroom. She sat on the edge of the bed. Her eyes dropped to the backs of her hands resting on her knees, pleased to note no sun damage. She enjoyed wearing flattering figure-hugging clothes and the admiration that went with it but was equally comfortable in boots, jeans and cotton shirts. She ran her hands over her smooth cheeks and forehead then clawed her fingers to run through her honey-blonde hair, lightly massaging her skull. As her fingers slipped to the end of the silky strands, she flicked them in front of her eyes smugly noting so few grey ones. She wondered complacently if the absence of age lines was because she was a wealthy, well-known horse breeder, a success.

I know I rub some people up the wrong way, she mused, *but there's no harm in being decisive, it gets things done. I'm determined and persistent and I can use charm or gritty resolution, whatever works to get my way. I'm successful and proud of it.*

She frowned, realising that once again she was thinking only of herself, not including her husband in her reflections. It reinforced her earlier idea that she was quite content, glad not to have him here contradicting her, not missing him in the least. She shrugged carelessly, dismissing him from her mind.

Opening the drawer of the bedside table, she withdrew a small, white box and extracted a single-use prefilled syringe. She tore open an alcohol wipe and, lifting her blouse, swabbed her flat belly. She injected the contents of the syringe and disposed of it in the sharps container, her face registering distaste for the unattractive yellow container. She closed the white box and replaced it in the drawer. Walking into the ensuite, she took a packet of sedatives from the vanity drawer and extracted a tablet from the foil.

Felicity slid the unused tablets in foil back into the pack and tossed it back in the drawer, pushing it shut. She popped the tablet in her mouth and washed it down with a mouthful of water. Finally, she walked back into the kitchen and rinsed the wine glass, upending it in the drainer. Glancing at the clock, she reminded herself the instructions for the tablets were to "take one tablet, half to three-quarters of an hour before retiring for the night". *Just enough time for a last check of the stables to be sure all is in order for the night,* she thought.

As she walked along the garden path, Felicity gazed with proprietary pride at the canopy of stars twinkling in the wide southern sky. *They shine above my land,* she thought smugly. A sudden shiver reminded her that winter was barely over, quickly chilling the night air, and she lengthened her stride. Arriving at the entry to the vast stable barn, Felicity paused to allow her eyes to adjust to the deep gloom inside. She smiled contentedly, hearing the reassuring soft rustles of the horses' sleepy movements in their stalls. More from memory than actual sight, she walked down the centre aisle, smelling the familiar mixture of horse feed and horses, listening for signs of unrest. A gentle wicker acknowledged her presence, and she relaxed, knowing that all was well.

Suddenly, Felicity doubled over, gasping with vicious, twisting stomach cramps. She staggered a couple of steps gripping her belly. Through the blinding pain, she felt herself tumbling and threw out a hand to soften her fall. On the barn floor, she barely registered the feel of the sawdust on her cheek as she struggled to draw breath, gasping again and again as she writhed in agony. Her back arched as she managed to draw one final breath before death halted her spasming muscles and her heart.

A short time later, the gloom was broken by torchlight flicking from side to side on the barn floor, keeping time with the owner's casual walk. As the new arrival advanced into the barn, the beam of light passed over the small still form on the sawdust, then snapped back to it. A soft exclamation, quickened footsteps, the light sharply focused on the body. The interloper stood still, watching carefully for signs of life. Felicity's chest didn't rise or fall; her face was pale, eyes unfocused. No move was made to touch or revive her. Finally, the watcher exhaled decisively and quickly stepped to the utility space at the end of the barn, selecting a long-handled pitchfork. A few quick strides back to the body and the pitchfork was thrust with sudden savage force into Felicity's back.

'Take that, you hard-hearted control freak! And good riddance!'

The torch beam swung round, and its owner confidently left the barn. The horses continued their gentle movements, undisturbed by the body or the actions of the intruder.

* * *

Detective Sergeant (plain clothes) Kaylee Bradshaw stretched luxuriously, lazily assessing the morning temperature. She concluded that despite it being very early spring, there was still enough winter in the air to make snuggling in bed as long as possible very appealing. She sighed regretfully, mentally running over office tasks she knew were waiting and began prioritising and allocating them to various staff members.

Suddenly, shrilly, the phone intruded. Kaylee smiled when she saw the caller: Ben Wharton. He wasn't a bad second fiddle in their duo. Smart, ambitious, easy on the eye. Ben was good at thinking outside the box and had been long enough in the area to have developed a strong local knowledge.

'Hey, Ben, what's happening?'

'Get out of bed, lazy bones. There's been a suspicious death up the valley on one of the horse studs.' Ben's voice was cheerful but businesslike. 'You coming in, or will I pick you up on my way out there?'

'Pick me up in ten and grab me a coffee, please.'

She disconnected and threw back the scarlet doona. As she swished through the shower, Kaylee mused on her good fortune at landing in a new rural promotion and having someone like Ben to help her ease into being familiar with the job and location. They had fallen into a comfortable working relationship in a short space of time. Ben seemed to know when it was okay to kid around but always sensed immediately the right time to drop the horse play and work seriously. She dressed quickly, sliding into a pink and grey fleece. She was just pulling her damp dark hair into a ponytail when Ben blew the horn out the front. Grabbing her keys and bag, she slammed the front door behind her and leapt down the stairs two at a time. As she seated herself in the passenger seat, she gave Ben a sidelong glance while she clicked her seatbelt in. He was dressed neatly but casually, holding out the coffee mug. Kaylee liked that his appearance was so deceptive: he always looked very much the laid-back Aussie but could be relied on to be as alert as a hunting tiger, taking in all sorts of details and storing them for later analysis.

'Thanks for the coffee,' she said, taking the disposable mug. 'Fill me in on what you know, Benny boy.'

'Lucky you've got me for the brains in the partnership. You look like a galah in that fleece!' Ben grinned slyly. Kaylee had a small private smile, pleased that he'd noticed her appearance. Then he spoke economically, his eyes on the road. 'I like this valley, small and picturesque. Not crowded with flashy showcase studs, one after the perfect other. Quaint village too, Wheeler. We're heading to Divine Hayfields, last farm in the valley.'

'Okay, thanks for the travelogue,' she smart-mouthed. 'Now, what happened up there?'

'Looks like the owner, one Mrs Felicity Hathaway, has been stabbed in the back with a pitchfork.'

Kaylee choked on a mouthful of coffee. 'Good grief,' she spluttered, 'and it killed her?'

'Looks like it,' Ben nodded.

'Rough stuff. Who found her?'

'Jarred Green, the manager. He called it in. He found her on the floor of the stable building when he went in to start the day. He's been working there for about fifteen years.'

'Well, I guess that'll do for starters. That sounds really violent, a lot of pent-up anger.' Kaylee paused, thinking. 'How many people living or working up there?' she added.

'Not quite sure. Mr and Mrs Hathaway are big names in the district, it's a large and profitable stud and they're seen in all the right places. They have a son and daughter both still living at home but past school age. Then there'd be a handful of stable lads and farm hands, a horse breaker, probably a mechanic.'

'Why would anyone want to kill someone so prominent? This won't be an open-and-shut thing, will it?'

They drove in silence and presently reached Wheeler. Free from concentrating on driving, Kaylee looked with interest at the small village. She saw a general store with a petrol pump, a small, neat primary school, bakery, a beautiful but ancient church with hall attached and a few houses. Ben carried on his commentary. He told her the houses were mainly inhabited by people who worked on nearby farms or were contract rural workers. The school principal lived in a cottage in the school grounds and supplemented the school enrolment with three children of his own, with the remaining numbers made up of children from within the village and farms around. The church and adjoining hall, despite being of such an age as to qualify for the term 'historical', still functioned, regularly providing a popular venue for weddings, christenings, and funerals for those of Church of England persuasion. The vicar lived close to the church and recognised the value of his church hall as a community centre that drew one and all. To this end, he customarily rented out the hall to almost anyone for almost anything. The monthly markets were held there, and the local Country Women's Association used it for their meetings, as did the Rural Fire Service and the pre-school playgroup.

Ben steered the four-wheel drive confidently along the right fork of the road in the village. He checked the rear vision mirror and noted with satisfaction the forensic van following.

Arriving at the horse stud, Kaylee took in the well-ordered paddocks contrasting sharply with the surrounding rugged mountains. Ben drove straight to the stables, bypassing the elegant old homestead, closely followed by the other vehicle. He switched off the engine, and they walked across a short expanse of clipped grass towards the wide stable doors. The two police officers, tall and well-built, stepped from the daylight into the restful neutral light of the vast stable building. Equine heads looked over each stable half-door, ears pricked towards the strangers. Kaylee and Ben stared back for a while as their eyes adjusted to the dim light. Ahead, in the centre walkway, was what looked like a carelessly discarded crumpled chaff bag.

Kaylee led the way towards the object, with Ben a short way behind. They stopped at the small slim woman lying sprawled in the centre aisle. A rusted ancient pitchfork grotesquely impaled her back. Despite her years of experience, Kaylee turned cold.

Jarred Green saw the officers silhouetted in the doorway.

Slowly, reluctantly he went to meet them from deep within the stable where he had been standing diffidently with some of the staff. It seemed to him mere moments before that he had walked cheerfully towards the stables, enjoying the soft morning sunlight that promised another warm early spring day. He'd been preoccupied planning the first task of the day, namely supervising the lads as they started their job of mucking out the stables for their expensive four-footed inhabitants.

Where better to work, he had mused, reflecting yet again on his good fortune when, fifteen years ago, he landed the job of manager for the famous Divine Hayfields horse stud. He worked every day with the animals he had loved since he was little. Sure, it was difficult at times working for the Hathaways, because they were forever arguing about the running of the place. But eventually they agreed long enough to give him their directions and listen to his input.

Now this disaster! One of them dead! Hell!

He forced his shoulders back holding out his hand to the male cop. 'Jarred Green.'

Ben shook his hand, muttering, 'Senior Constable Ben Wharton,' then turning towards Kaylee he said clearly, 'Detective Sergeant Kaylee Bradshaw.'

'Jarred. A hard morning for you,' Kaylee commented giving him a brief handshake. 'We could talk outside, I think.' She watched the forensic photographer and her assistant settle to their tasks for a moment then led the way out of the stables.

Jenny Mumford moved slowly through the task of evidence gathering with her camera. Short and tending slightly towards over-weight, she was born and educated in England. She was highly skilled in the field of forensic photography, but no amount of talent could prevent the application of such an obvious nickname as "Clicks". She didn't mind, it seemed to signify to her that she was an accepted part of the team. She worked well with her partner, Dave Hogan, commonly known as Paul, and often grinned to herself about their names. So typical in Australia to have quirky or offbeat nicknames. She applied herself to the task at hand, meticulously photographing. Dave dropped to one knee, eyes scanning the ground and the body for anything unusual or significant.

Kaylee spoke again as they walked into the sunlight, 'Might as well leave Clicks and Paul to get on with it.'

From the stable door, it was easy to see the valley stretch away to the north. Behind the stable the characteristic cliffs that feature in many valleys in the Upper Hunter rose, creating a sheer secure wall curving around three sides of the farm. In some places there was no need for fencing, so steep were the cliffs. The homestead nestled snugly in the curve, a short distance behind and to the left of the stables. Large formal gardens complimented the elegant old building, and a tennis court was visible at the far end of the house.

'How about you give us a bit of background, Jarred. That'll get the ball rolling and then we can ask any questions that arise,' Ben said casually.

Kaylee leant on the stable wall while she listened. She was a strong woman, both physically and mentally, dedicated to her career. During her rise through the ranks to her current position, she had needed strength and tenacity just to prove her competence in a world that was still inclined to favour men over women. As a result, she was well-known for her determination and success in solving crimes. She firmly believed in making sure junior officers were given exposure to as much variety as possible in policing. She made sure that they were fully supported and encouraged to develop confidence in taking initiative in every investigation. Her confidence in her own ability enabled her to share her knowledge and experience productively with those less experienced. Even though it was her habit to help other officers gain experience, Kaylee also kept in mind that she could learn from others. She looked thoughtfully at Ben's intent face.

Jarred gazed out across the peaceful paddocks, listening to the call of the butcherbirds greeting the day. He squared his shoulders then began speaking, hesitantly at first, letting his ideas roll out as they occurred to him. He described bits of the last fifteen years because he couldn't bring himself to talk about the here and now just yet.

'Since beginning this job, I quickly recognised Mrs Hathaway's determination to be involved in running the farm with her husband. She inherited it from her father. She loves, loved being part of the day-to-day routine and the decision-making. She fully understood the workings of the farm, but her decisions were impulsive, often impractical, based on instinct and her own whims, rather than knowledge from research. She could be pretty outspoken, so of course there were frequent clashes between her and Mr Hathaway, Gordon. He's knowledgeable and experienced in all elements of horse husbandry and his decisions are based on strong, good sense ...'

'Keep going, this is good,' Kaylee prodded gently. She watched Ben processing Jarred's words. She knew Ben's easy-going, cheerful character made him look casual but she understood how seriously he took his job. On a previous occasion, he had surprised her with ideas that were outside the norm but were curiously accurate. She considered his odd insight an asset to cultivate.

'They're both intelligent, forceful people, an attractive couple but frequently at odds with each other.' Jarred shrugged. 'It was sometimes frustrating, their personality clashes, but I usually enjoyed my job.' His voice faltered, 'But this! This is shocking. Its way beyond my experience. At first, I thought someone had left a chaff bag on the ground. Then I saw it was her. I didn't know what to do, so I felt for a pulse. Nothing. Her skin was quite cold. I dialled triple zero and went to the door to stop the stable lads from coming in. I told them to come in the side door down the back.'

'You did exactly right,' murmured Kaylee. 'Why would someone want to kill her? Does anyone spring to mind who would have attacked Mrs Hathaway this way?'

Jarred hesitated again. 'Well, she would have got under everyone's skin at some time or other. She even managed to upset Vicar Aligardy from the church!!'

'Interesting. Have you got other jobs you can give the lads to keep them out of the stables until the forensic team are done?'

'The horses need feeding and watering. Can't leave them

too long,' Jarred said apologetically, his stress level rising again.

A thought suddenly occurred to Kaylee. 'How come Mrs Hathaway was out and about this early and not Mister?' she asked bluntly.

'Mr Hathaway's in Perth. He left yesterday morning. I think he was going to be away about a week,' Jarred replied.

'Who else is here?' Ben asked.

'Susannah and Darren Hathaway, or among us all, Zanna and Dar. They're the grown-up family. Susannah's done an animal husbandry course and supposed to be getting experience here before moving to Queensland to work. Darren's a computer nerd doesn't do anything but computers. He set up the stud books electronically and maintains the programs for the business, the stud books and staff pay and so on. Saves them quite a bit on admin fees, although I'm sure they pay him.'

'Well, I guess we'll go and break the news to them. Our guys shouldn't be too long in your stable. Who opens the big end doors each day?'

'In mild weather like this we don't shut them at night. The horses like the fresh air and so long as it's not frosty or a howling wind, they're warm enough in their stables.'

'So much for security! OK, Jarred, thanks. We'll get on over to the house then. A vehicle will soon arrive to take Mrs Hathaway to the mortuary once Clicks and Paul are done. When we finish at the house, we'll want to interview you and your boys so tell them to hold off going out to any paddock jobs.'

'Right,' Jarred turned, ready to go, then paused. 'I don't

have to let Mr Hathaway know, do I? You'll do that, won't you?'

'Yes,' Kaylee responded, 'That's our job. We'll wait a bit though. It's still pretty early in Perth, round four thirty, I'd think.'

'Thanks,' Jarred muttered and walked back to the stable lads. 'Come on, then. Better get to work.' He jerked his head, beckoning them to the path along the outside of the barn.

In a quiet group, they walked through the trees behind the stables down towards the feed and tack sheds and the stable rear entry, avoiding the forensic team and their distasteful task.

'What'll this mean for us, Jarred?' asked Hamish. He had been standing quietly by listening to his workmates with a troubled frown. He looked continually to Jarred as if seeking reassurance. At nineteen he was the youngest of the workers, shy and introverted but clearly upset by this morning's event. He was good with horses, calm and steady but he had yet to develop confidence in dealing with peers. He was an easy target for the others, especially Kevin who was short-tempered and edgy. Hamish was liked, not necessarily admired, by the other lads. If Jarred was asked to pass a criticism of him, it was that Hamish lacked initiative.

'We'll just have to get on with things as usual, at least until Mr Hathaway gets back. But I don't know what will happen after that.' Jarred spoke slowly, thinking of the long-term implications. He wasn't sure whether Mrs Hathaway had included her husband in a joint ownership situation when she inherited or what the legal situation was.

'We just start mucking out then, hey?' Taj Papali spoke with the upward inflection common to those with origins in New Zealand. Not much managed to upset his easy-going nature and he took all life's hiccups with a cheerfully philosophical attitude. Maybe being one in a family of twelve contributed to his relaxed view of life. He was content being paid to do a reasonably undemanding job and enjoyed working with horses. He was a sociable person who enjoyed being among others and rarely let their personalities rub him up the wrong way.

'Yeah, we just start mucking out, hey.' Kevin Craig spoke in an unpleasant mimic, frowning out from under his curly red hair. 'Of course we get started! The horses won't do their own stalls, will they?' His tone was impatient. As the specialist groom for Divine Madam, the most valuable breeding mare at the stud, he thought himself superior to the other three grooms and treated them with endless intolerance. Jarred found his chip on the shoulder mindset rather hard to put up with but had to admit Kevin did a thoroughly good job of caring for the mare.

Mac Brennan, the fourth of the lads, was a taciturn local. He didn't stay with the other lads in the cottage but drove up daily from Wheeler where he lived with his wife and small son. His start time was geared so he could finish mid-afternoon to mind his son after school while his wife worked at the general store.

'Okay, fellers, we can't get on with it until they finish in there. So the horses will have to wait. Taj, you, Mac and Hamish go to the feed shed and start preparing the feed buckets. Kevin, you come with me,' Jarred headed towards the tack shed. He paused and listened to the sounds in the stable. It was quiet, not reflecting the violent scene inside. He was a little surprised at how calm the horses were; usually when their routine was disturbed some of them could get quite fidgety. He wondered how long the deceptively peaceful atmosphere would continue.

CHAPTER TWO

I t seems strange ...' Ben began, slowly letting his thoughts form. He liked to picture his brain as a series of sieves, the first one catching the big clues and then sifting down to the final one that caught the really tiny but important clues. 'I can't see it. You've got a pitchfork coming into her back when she's standing up. She wouldn't have fallen like that. And not much blood. I reckon she was already on the ground and then she was stuck with the fork. But there was no sign of a struggle on the ground. I don't get it.'

'Yeah. Clicks will get all the details,' Kaylee spoke confidently. 'You can pursue that thought when we get back to the station and look at the pictures from all angles.' She paused, thinking about the next part of the process, then gave herself a tiny shake. 'Well, I guess we'd better get on with telling the family.'

Sergeant Bradshaw may have been strong, but she was not an unfeeling woman and, to her, telling next of kin about the death of a loved one was probably the least pleasant aspect of her job. She beckoned the stud manager who was standing indecisively with Kevin. Jarred immediately walked over, eyebrows raised.

'Do you have any idea why Mr Hathaway was in Perth?'

'No idea at all, I'm afraid,' the manager replied quietly.

'Okay.' She waved him away and turned towards the house, reaching for her phone. She made a call to the station.

During the call, she briefly outlined the situation on the farm. She asked for the Registrar at Muswellbrook Courts to locate a forensic pathologist to perform the autopsy and made a formal request for liaison with the Perth police so they had details and could support Mr Hathaway if necessary. She made a mental note to get his contact details from one of his children. She added a reminder to offer Mr Hathaway assistance in making arrangements for his speedy return to New South Wales.

She ended the call and hurried to catch up with Ben as he walked along the covered pathway towards the house. The gardens were attractive and well maintained.

'All this, and I guess they've got a gardener too,' murmured Ben waving his arm expansively.

The front door was open, but they paused on the threshold. Kaylee knocked, 'Anybody up? Susannah? Darren? It's the police. We need to talk to you.'

Susannah Hathaway lean and long limbed, came without hurry, a puzzled, slightly irritated expression on her face.

'Why are you here? Where's Mum? Can't she deal with this?' She sounded like a spoilt brat and looked very much as if she'd just woken up. Her tangled blonde hair was dragged back in a ponytail, her T-shirt and jeans rumpled. She beckoned the police to follow and walked into the kitchen with the long easy strides of those who are accustomed to plenty of space to move in. She was much taller than her mother had appeared, and Ben judged her to be round twenty-three or twenty-four. She showed she wasn't totally self-absorbed by putting on the kettle and setting out cups.

Kaylee glanced into the lounge on the right, shook her head, and followed Susannah into the kitchen. Ben followed more slowly, taking in the expensive modern decor. Outside, the house looked like a traditional old homestead but inside it had received a makeover of severe proportions. Evidently no expense had been spared but to Ben's mind, all the charm hinted at on the outside had been lost in the transformation. He didn't like all the shiny, cold, stark black and white. He heard bare feet padding on the tiled floor and looked towards the interior of the house, but nobody materialised, and he continued into the kitchen.

Susannah's next words indicated a strong-willed nature that reflected her mother's more than she realised.

'Well?' Now you've woken me up. What?'

'Can we wait 'til your brother's here, please?' Detective Bradshaw's tone was lowkey.

Susannah gave a quick gesture of irritation and went to the kitchen door. 'Darren! Get out here! Hurry up.' A door slammed and she nodded, satisfied her brother was on his way. She turned back to the two police officers. 'Tea? Coffee?'

'I'm right thanks,' said Ben.

'I'll have coffee, white, no sugar, thanks,' Kaylee responded.

'What's the matter? Why aren't you talking to Mum?' Darren appeared sleepily in the kitchen doorway clad in a startling bright-patterned robe. He too was tall and slender but less assertive than his sister. His round glasses frames gave him an air of defencelessness. Even at twenty-one, he was clearly accustomed to his mother being very much in evidence and totally in control.

The kettle boiled and Susannah made coffees for Kaylee and herself. She didn't bother to ask Darren what he wanted, just fixed him a weak herbal tea and pushed it towards him.

'I'm Detective Sergeant Kaylee Bradshaw, and this is Detective Senior Constable Ben Wharton,' Kaylee began. 'We actually need to talk to you about your Mum. There's no easy way to say this to you. I'm afraid your mother has been killed.'

Susannah paled and looked quickly at Darren. He sagged back against the bench and put his hand to his mouth.

'An accident?' Susannah's voice rose sharply.

'No. This wasn't an accident, I'm afraid.'

'What do you mean?' Concern was beginning to show on Susannah's face as the news sank in.

'We're going to have to treat this as a homicide from the evidence at the scene.' The detective spoke quietly and without emphasis. 'Can we ask you both some questions?'

'Oh, God! What about Dad?' Susannah's quavering voice betrayed how thin her veneer of confidence was.

'Well, it'll be a bit early in Perth just yet. Would you like to break the news, or would you prefer us to do it? We need to see about getting him back here as soon as possible. What was he over there for?' Ever alert for any tiny clue, Ben watched Susannah's face closely.

Susannah's jaw tightened and she said flatly, 'His sister, our Aunt Linda, lives there. She, um, wanted help for something.' Her voice dropped. 'I don't think I can tell him, but you can't either. He never answers calls from unknown numbers. Stupid habit. You can always just hang up and block the number, but he doesn't get that.' After a pause, she went on in a stronger voice. 'You can ring Aunt Linda,' adding coldly, 'she can tell him.'

'Can you give us Linda's surname and phone number? I take it he's staying with her. It'll save time when we try to contact him,' Ben said.

'Sure. It's Frazer-Baines,' Susannah replied curtly. She opened her phone and scrolled through the contacts stopping at the entry named Aunt Linda. She slowly recited the number which Ben jotted in his notebook.

Darren hadn't spoken at all. Just stood there looking blankly out the kitchen window.

'Why Mum? Can I see her?' Susannah asked in a small, tightly controlled voice.

'I'll take you,' Ben volunteered. 'She's in the stables.'

The pitchfork had been removed and her mother placed on her back in the body bag, zipped up to her neck. Her face was pale and peaceful, carrying no hint of how her life ended. Susannah took a long, grim look and then gently laid her hand on her mother's forehead. She sighed deeply and straightened up. She looked slowly round the stable building as if seeking reassurance that not everything had changed irrevocably. Then she straightened her shoulders, turned and walked towards the big doors and the sunshine.

Susannah Hathaway stood beside Ben outside the stables.

Her shoulders were still straight but much of her assurance was gone and her face was strained. She gazed around the sweep of the valley.

'Did you know my great-grandfather called this place Wheeler Park? Wheeler was his surname. He loved that there was a big W formation in the cliffs back there.' She waved her arm back towards the sheer cliffs that featured two clefts resembling a letter W. 'It was like he had the only place that had a physical representation of his name. Mum changed the name to Divine Hayfields when she inherited it from Grandfather, her dad. She figured the quality of the horses would stand no matter what the place was called. She said she wanted the stud to reflect her, not Grandfather. But she wasn't really a 'divine' sort of person. She was too sarcastic. Even if she said you looked 'divine' you felt that she probably meant there was a caterpillar on your collar or some butter and toast crumbs on your cheek. I don't know why she was like that, really. Grandfather was lovely and gentle, and he was simply happy to own horses that were successful. But she liked to be in control ...' Susannah's voice trailed off and she took a deep slow breath. 'Who would do that to her? I mean, she *did* manage to upset pretty well everyone but not to that extent, surely.'

'So, you can't think of anyone who would dislike her enough to kill her?' Ben's green eyes seemed focused on the valley, but he carefully watched Susannah out of the corner of his eye.

'Everyone was mad at her for something. She and Dad fought all the time but he's not here and anyway he wouldn't, would he? I think they loved each other. It just didn't show when they were shouting at each other.'

'Did you and your mother get on OK?' Ben reasoned that he might as well get the questions asked while she seemed to be keeping herself together.

Susannah's face darkened under a frown. 'Yeah, we got on just fine.'

Hmm, a bit more there than she's letting on, Ben thought.

'What about Jarred?' Ben ventured.

'Jarred? You *are* joking! He loves his job here. There's no way he'd put that in jeopardy, no matter how many times she contradicted what Dad said and sent him on wild goose chases!'

Ben stored that up to revisit with Jarred later. He thought that life at Divine Hayfields was far from serene and decided that this may turn out to be quite a complicated investigation.

'What about Darren?' he probed.

'Darren? Ha! Nobody bothers Dar and Dar doesn't bother anybody. So long as nothing gets between him and his computers, he's fine.' Susannah's answer didn't display much sensitivity for her brother. Ben decided from Susannah's attitude towards her brother that he wouldn't get much more from her in that direction.

In the kitchen, Kaylee eyed Darren's back speculatively. He was staring out the window, standing straight but not rigidly so.

'So, Darren, your Mum ran the place, did she?' Kaylee posed the provocative question in a deliberately neutral tone.

'She wished! She wanted to run everything. Everyone's life, the farm, the village, the church! Control! That should have been her middle name. But there are some things she just couldn't control and God how she hated that!' he burst out.

'What couldn't she control?' Kaylee prodded.

'Me! Yeah, me. Quiet little Darren, the computer nerd! That's all they think of me. No personality, no feelings, nothing but downloads and uploads, apps and installations. They only think of me in terms of stuff that can help them with the business. Well, they're so wrong! There's a whole lot more to me and she didn't like finding THAT out.' He whirled towards Kaylee, his face defiant.

'What didn't she like finding out, Darren?'

He turned a ghastly sneering smile on Kaylee, his folded his arms holding his vivid robe closed.

'They weren't going to get an heir to carry on the farm from me! And there'd be no kudos in having me around if I lived as I want to. Huh, they'd be laughed at, shamed, in the horse circles! Sure we live in a progressive age but that hasn't quite extended this far up the Hunter Valley. It's killing them all knowing I'm gay but *she* really hated it!' he concluded triumphantly.

Darren's bravado crumbled as he finished his dramatic announcement. His eyes filled with tears and he turned abruptly back to the window.

CHAPTER THREE

Kaylee's face was thoughtful. She frowned briefly as the phone rang.

'I'll get that, will I, Darren?' she said coolly as she reached for the warbling little piece of technology.

'Sergeant Bradshaw speaking.'

'Hello? Susannah? Get your father on the bloody phone will you!'

'This isn't Susannah. Its Sergeant Bradshaw.'

'What? Hello? Hello? God, a bloody wrong number!'

The phone went dead in Kaylee's hands.

'Well, Darren. Who might that have been? Loud voice, rapid fire, swears, doesn't listen.'

'Burt Bunrack.' Darren didn't even have to think about it. Before Kaylee could ask any more, the phone rang again.

This time she spoke slowly and clearly. 'This is Sergeant Bradshaw from Muswellbrook Police at Divine Hayfields. Good morning. Who is speaking?'

'Eh? Is that you Felicity?' came the puzzled impatient voice.

'No. This is *Sergeant Bradshaw*,' Kaylee repeated slowly and clearly. 'Is that Burt Bunrack?'

'Er, yes. I was looking for Gordon.'

'He's in Perth. So, you can talk to me if you can spare a minute.'

'Well, you'd better make it quick, I'm a busy man.' It didn't take Burt long to slip back to his loud, edgy, phone manner.

'What is your address, Mr Bunrack?'

'I own Croham, the farm next door to Divine Hayfields. Damn stupid name! I want to know what Gordon's timetable is for the wetland rehabilitation. And now he's gone off to bloody Perth. Typical! The bugger only thinks about himself. Never mind that I have to run my place as well as fit in with him.'

'Could we call in and see you on our way back to town?' Kaylee thought it very strange that Burt hadn't even asked what the police were doing at Divine Hayfields. *Maybe he's just totally self-absorbed or half nuts,* she thought. He sounded half nuts. She gave herself a frown for such an unprofessional thought.

'Oh, well, call in all you like. I may or may not be around. Is that all you want?' he asked ungraciously.

'Yes, thank you Mr Bunrack. We'll see you later,' Kaylee said and hung up the phone.

She turned to Darren. 'Maybe you can fill in some of the blanks for me. Mr Bunrack wasn't exactly helpful.'

'He never is. He doesn't listen to anyone, just goes on like a bulldozer. The only thing that stops him is his wife. Then he shuts up and listens! Her parents had a winery down near Cessnock and he met her when he was working there to pay his way through ag college. He has the farm next door. They run Angus cattle and have a sort of a boutique market garden specialising in foods that complement the beef. Then they sell directly to restaurants in Sydney. Make a fortune. None of your saleyard stuff for them. Pretty well straight from paddock to plate. You have to hand it to him, even though he can be a really prickly pig of a neighbour, he's a pretty good farmer. He's got a good business head but for some reason, he can't get his head around mobile phones. Doesn't trust them. Weird really because he's quite happy to use all the other farming tech available. I think his wife gave him the idea for the market garden. Gisella, she's Italian, very fiery.'

Kaylee was happy to let Darren talk, it seemed to relax him after his outburst and his information was plentiful and helpful. He seemed quite observant and rather skilled at character analysis.

'Family?' she prompted.

'Oh they only have a son. Silvio. Totally doted on especially by his mum. He's twenty-six, pretty clever, good looking, in a smooth sort of way. Went to boarding school in Sydney. But that's nothing wonderful, so did Susannah and I. He did landscape gardening at college but he's just working on the farm at the moment. He does most of the garden stuff under *Mother's* orders, of course. But Burt has the final say in everything.'

'How'd Burt get on with your parents?'

'Pretty well, really. I mean when you think how impatient he is and what a control freak Mum is ... was.' Darren faltered, then carried on. 'He and Dad were working together to rehabilitate the wetlands. It's not really a wetland, just a flat area where the creek spreads out.

It's been over-cleared and over-grazed and it's getting eroded, just a useless patch of weeds. So, Dad and Burt decided to fence it off and plant some river red gums and she-oaks to stabilise the banks. They've put up a temporary fence, but Burt's cranky because he wants to get on with his bit of permanent fencing. Dad hasn't decided exactly where to put the fence. Well, that's not really true. Mum and Dad haven't, hadn't *agreed* about where to put the fence. Burt had a real shouting match with Mum about it the other day. But she told him 'no jumped-up old Pommy' was going to tell her how to run her farm and walked off. You should have seen his face!' Darren smiled at the memory.

'Mmm. We'll be calling on Mr Bunrack later this morning,' Kaylee said.

'What? You don't think he did it, do you?' Darren jumped slightly, his face pale.

'Why not? You said she'd made him very angry.'

'Yeah, but not Burt. It can't be him, no, not Burt!' Darren's voice rose.

'Why so certain, Darren?' Kaylee willed herself to stay still, but she felt her pulse increase sharply, along with her curiosity.

'Oh, well, you know ...' Darren spread his hands and shrugged.

Footsteps on the entry tiles drew the attention of both Darren and the detective.

'You ready to interview the stable lads? They're getting on with cleaning out the stables.' Ben poked his tousled head around the kitchen door. Kaylee sighed. *Not the best timing in the world, Ben, I was just getting somewhere,* she thought.

'Yeah, I guess the day is wasting and they've got things to get on with. Darren, thank you very much. You've been most helpful. We'll talk some more later,' Kaylee smiled reassuringly at Darren.

She turned and set off after Ben who was already striding back across the entry towards the front door and the increasingly warm day outside. As they left the house, Darren trailed slowly towards his bedroom. The sound of the message notification on his mobile quickened his steps. He snatched up the phone and scanned the brief message: *What did you do?*

His texted reply was a silent scream: *NOTHING. NOTHING AT ALL!*

Out in the sunshine, Kaylee turned to Ben, 'Did you get much out of Susannah?'

'She and her mother weren't exactly best buds but family loyalty isn't letting her expand on that at this stage. And you saw her reaction when I asked why her dad was in Perth. Did Darren have anything to say?'

'As a matter of fact, it was quite revealing talking to Darren. He's very observant and rather underrated by the whole family, I feel. We also have to talk to the neighbours, a Mr Burt Bunrack and his family. Can do that on our way back to the station.'

They strode in the direction of the tack shed where they had last seen Jarred disappearing with Kevin. Through the open door they saw the manager and Kevin sorting halters, bridles and other tack.

'These can go to the saddler in Muswellbrook for repairs next time you go in,' Jarred said to Kevin.

'Right, Boss.' Kevin turned to see whose shadow had darkened the doorway.

'Ah, Jarred,' Ben spoke, 'can you get the lads together so we can have a chat with them?'

'Yeah, they're in the feed shed. Let's go down there.'

Jarred led the way. Ben walked beside Kevin, taking in the details of his neat appearance and latest in farm workwear. He said conversationally to Kevin, 'So, you like working here, Kevin?'

'It has its ups and downs.' As usual when he was stressed, Kevin felt tongue-tied and clumsy.

'The ups?' Ben prodded gently.

'The horses.'

Wow, this guy is hard going, Ben thought, lapsing into silence.

'Okay, guys, we're going to try not to take up too much more of your time. We realise you have work waiting,' Kaylee spoke while the men seated themselves on hay bales and upturned feed bins.

'Jarred, about what time did you go into the stables to start work?'

'We're all usually well and truly started by half-six most mornings. I got there about six this morning.'

'Who was next to arrive?'

'We all walked down together. Mac was driving up just as we got to the stable,' Taj offered.

'Do you guys all live up here?'

The questions continued for about half an hour. Jarred

described the living arrangements for himself and the live-in lads in a cottage located behind the feed shed-cum-office. Horse feed was stored in large bins in the main part of the shed and off to the side was a spartan office Jarred used, as well as a bathroom for the convenience of all staff. In the office were a couple of hard chairs, a telephone, and a desk with computer, linked to the main one Darren used at the homestead. On one wall, there was a large lockable cabinet where various horse treatments and accessories were stored. Along the other wall was a bench with electric jug, mugs, and coffee. Under the bench was a bar fridge with milk, a few bottles of beer and horse medications requiring refrigeration.

'Are you working towards any important deadlines or is this the routine for the whole year?' Ben asked.

'The official birthday for all horses is August first. We aim to foal as soon as possible after that date. Any foals born before August first are classed as one-year-olds on August one, which puts them way behind those born just after August who will turn one in twelve months' time. Does that make sense?' Ben and Kaylee nodded. Jarred continued. 'Mares are joined to the stallion immediately after foaling. Mares are either sent away to stallions and have their foals at the stallion's stud or foal at their home stud if it has a stallion. Sometimes studs use artificial insemination, saves the expense of a stallion and the wear and tear of travel on the mares. The mares and their foals are brought back to their home stud once the mares are mated. Yearlings are generally sold round September or October. So, things are quite busy from August to November. After that, it's just routine training, feeding, care, farm maintenance. We grow some crops for fodder for the winter. Paddocks need to be mulched, fences repaired, that type of thing.'

'Have all your mares dropped their foals now?'

'A couple that were sent away are still to foal, but we're all done here. Working towards the yearling sales. Ours is due in ten weeks' time, a bit later than usual. We were a bit late organising an auctioneer and he was booked up earlier.'

'Right, so the next big thing is your sale. Could Mrs Hathaway have been murdered in connection with that?'

Jarred wrinkled his brow, 'I don't see why. I can't see how her death would seriously impact the sale or the outcome. After all, Mr Hathaway can run the place.'

Jarred continued with his description of Divine Hayfields routines. The Hathaway's had a housekeeper, Dell Sullivan, who lived in the village and came up daily, arriving round nine. Her duties included cleaning the main house, doing the laundry there and cleaning the cottage for the lads but they did their own cooking and laundry. She cooked for the Hathaways when they required but Felicity was reportedly quite happy to cook when she had time.

The lads had finished up their scheduled duties round five-thirty the previous evening. From there, Kevin said he'd gone for a long walk round the bottom of the cliffs. Like most workers with horses, Kevin was tall and slim. He was obviously fit but wiry rather than muscular. He seemed to be suppressing pent-up energy, either nervous or angry. He said he often walked at the end of the day. He could not find the words to add that it was difficult for him to fluently speak about his emotions and walking allowed him to burn off energy and bury thoughts he was unable to express.

The detectives continued with their questions. True to his laid-back nature, Taj had watched television and had a beer, happy to relax. A job was just a job to him, he was not afraid of hard work. So long as he was earning enough to support himself and send a little home to help his mother out, he was content.

Hamish said he'd put on a load of washing. He kept himself to himself and lay on his bed reading a magazine while the washing machine completed the cycle. Jarred said he'd done a final round of the stables about 5:45, then gone up to the main house to check with Mrs Hathaway about the next day's tasks. Taj had cooked the evening meal which they'd all eaten together around a quarter to seven. Then Hamish had cleared up and they all said they had either watched television or read in their rooms before turning in for the night.

Ben, listening carefully, decided there was plenty of room for any one of the lads to be out and about after dinner with no one being any the wiser. He made a mental note to check for more detail with each of them alone later.

CHAPTER FOUR

'How was Mrs Hathaway when you saw her yesterday evening?' Kaylee asked Jarred.

'Not too strung up, she didn't have Mr Hathaway to disagree with. But she couldn't make up her mind about anything. We were all pretty fed up by the end of the day because she'd had us going in circles all day. We don't have time for that time wasting.'

'I gather "strung up" is par for the course, is it?' Kaylee murmured.

'Yes, she's normally quite intense, planning training, who will be selling where and when. Then she second guesses herself and changes her plans but that's not too disastrous at this stage because it's still a couple of months 'til the next sale. We're training twelve yearlings for sale and breaking about twenty older horses that have been sold. It's often part of the sale contract to keep the horses on and train them for a fee.'

'A big workload for you guys.' Her stomach rumbled and she changed the subject. 'Who cooks for the staff?'

'We have a roster for all that. It's too messy and frustrating with everyone in the kitchen at once.'

Kaylee watched a car drive slowly up the road. 'Who would that be?'

Jarred glanced towards the road, 'Mrs Sullivan.'

'So, who is the trainer and where does he live? When does he work?' Kaylee returned to the investigation.

'Oh, that's Ali Hadji. He's from Syria, I think or Iraq, somewhere over there. He's a real wiz with horses ... he should have been here a while ago, actually.' Jarred frowned. 'He lives in the village, rents a house there.'

'Does anyone else work here?' Ben made rapid but accurate notes.

'Yeah, there's a guy called Jason, lives in the village. He lost his licence, too many speeding tickets. He usually gets a ride with Mrs Sullivan, probably with her now. Comes in when needed, helps with training under Ali's orders or does a bit of cultivation for Mr Hathaway when he wants it. Jason's pretty good with machinery so he services all the farm vehicles, too. He's coming every day for the next few weeks until we get the breaking done.'

'Okay, thanks guys. We'll leave it there. We have plenty to go on with. Can I ask that none of you leave the area without letting us know, until we get this all sorted out.' Ben closed and pocketed his notebook.

He and Kaylee walked to their vehicle, heads together, comparing notes in low voices.

'Where next, Boss?' Ben asked.

'We're visiting the Bunrack farm,' Kaylee's voice was firm. 'Timewise, it's probably not too early in Perth now. I'll just phone Aunt Linda and see if I can get onto Gordon.'

After a short drive back along the way they'd come, Ben turned in through two ornate lion-topped white gate pillars. A timber sign proclaimed Croham, in gold painted letters on a white background.

Ahead of them, a long, low white house could be seen. It had a red tiled roof and scarlet bougainvillea growing in wild profusion. Further along, a large orderly market garden stretched away to the left. Well-conditioned, glossy black cattle dotted the carefully fenced paddocks. As Kaylee and Ben exited the car, they could hear raised voices coming from in the house.

'... and how many more times do I have to say it, woman? We have more than enough to do! We're NOT going to branch out into desserts!' Mr Bunrack was shouting.

'Ahh Porca, how am I going to get it through that closed brain of yours? Burt Bunrack you are such an imbecile!' his wife shrieked.

'Anyone at home?' Kaylee projected her voice, causing a sudden silence inside. Then footsteps could be heard approaching the door. It opened to reveal a beautiful dark-haired woman, with a vibrant blue kaftan swirling about her shapely figure. Her cheeks were still an angry pink, but she attempted a welcoming face.

After Kaylee made the introductions, she and Ben were silently escorted through the cool, light house to a large open kitchen-cum-sunroom. The rear wall mostly consisted of windows and a pair of French doors which allowed an uninterrupted view of the gardens. Burt Bunrack was standing by the large dining table, scowling from under heavy reddish eyebrows. Gisella introduced the police and he hastily tried to look less annoyed. It was a habit from his wayward childhood back in England to reveal as little as possible to the police.

'I spoke to you earlier on the phone,' Kaylee said. She gestured inclusively towards Ben 'We were called to Divine Hayfields this morning because there has been a death.'

'Oh dio!' Gisella threw her hands over her face and rocked back and forwards.

'An accident? Who?'

'I'm sorry to tell you, it's Mrs Hathaway.'

Gisella let out a little scream. 'You could've broke it to her a bit gentler,' Burt growled moving to put an arm round his wife's shoulders. She shrugged him off impatiently, raising her face.

'What happened?' she quavered, with tears brimming in her eyes.

'Maybe we could start by checking up on where you were yesterday evening and last night. Is it just the two of you here?' Kaylee asked.

'Our son, Silvio, lives here with us. He's about somewhere,' Burt said.

'Outside, where he can't hear the shouting of his stubborn father,' Gisella spat, evidently unwilling to let Burt off easily. He glared at her and snapped, 'Maybe it would be 'elpful if you could find your precious son.'

Gisella flounced out through the French doors, 'Silvio caro, where are you?'

'What the 'ell's goin' on at that madhouse up the road? You thinkin' we've got somethin' to do with their trouble?' Burt hunched his shoulders and frowned. He was always uneasy when fighting with the very volatile Gisella because he wanted his own way without pushing her too far. Life was pretty good here in Australia, and Burt preferred it to stay that way.

'Let's wait for your wife and son, shall we?' Ben wanted the atmosphere as calm as possible.

Presently, Gisella returned with a tall, handsome young man. Silvio was well-built, muscular and fit without being bulky. He had inherited his mother's olive complexion and dark hair that crinkled thickly in a close crop. He had an open and friendly expression that made him extremely attractive. Introductions were made and Kaylee led off with a summary of the situation they had attended at the neighbouring farm. All three of the Bunrack family appeared genuinely shocked by the news of Felicity Hathaway's death as well as the manner of her death.

'So, Burt, what were you doing yesterday evening after about seven?'

'We 'ad dinner round then, Gisella and me and Silvio. We watched the news, little bit of comedy. Then we watched that new rescue drama. It was a double episode.'

Gisella nodded and said, 'We went to bed after that. Burt brings me cup of tea always about six in morning. Then I got up, knocked back the dough for the rolls. I put them in the oven.'

'I just wanted a quick look at that paddock we're rehabilitatin' to figure out where to put the fence. Bloody Gordon,' Burt's face reddened. 'Well, Gordon and Felicity still 'adn't made up their mind and I was gettin' sick of waitin'. I came back to the 'ouse and rang 'im. Got you instead.' He looked at Kaylee.

'What about you, Silvio. Were you watching telly with your folks?'

'Ah, no. Like Dad said, I had dinner with them, then I went out.'

Gisella pounced. 'I thought you in your room! Where you go? You not say nothing to me.'

'I just went out for a bit, Mama.'

'You not being honest with me! You want the police thinking you got something to hide? Where you go?'

Silvio's face flushed. He shrugged. 'Just out, Mama. No big deal. Walking, thinking, got home about eleven.'

Kaylee looked thoughtfully at Silvio. 'Did you go up to Divine Hayfields while you were walking?'

'No! I swear, never went near the place.' He threw up his hands and turned to the window.

Kaylee glanced at Ben. He gave a tiny nod. Together, they thanked the Bunracks for their cooperation and returned to the car.

'He'll keep,' Ben said.

CHAPTER FIVE

n the twelfth-floor suite of the Crowne Plaza hotel in Perth, Gordon Hathaway stretched and opened his eyes at his habitually early hour. He grinned with a feeling of intense well-being and glanced beside him at the cause. Antonia Larson's slim form was outlined beneath the sheet. Her face with flawless skin was centred in massed auburn curls. She slept peacefully with an arm crooked above her head.

He was convinced it was his lucky day when he met her that night in the bar. *What was it, ten months ago?* Wow, the time had flown and his necessary returns east to the stud dragged interminably. His sister Linda was a scatter-brained socialite with no sense for business. Her wealthy husband had died of the effects of his lavish lifestyle about five years ago and she'd quickly found herself in financial difficulties. Gordon had developed a rescue plan that was just on the right side of legal, but he had to make his presence felt in Perth on a regular basis or the plan could unravel unpleasantly. He didn't mind digging Linda out of trouble, but he refused to stay with her while he was in Perth. Staying at the Crowne was a luxury escape for him from the volcano that everyone else called living with Felicity. Antonia was the icing on the cake as far as he was concerned. His time with her was fantastic. They had so much in common. She was funny, supportive, strong and intelligent. One of the things he appreciated most about her was the total lack of meanness. She was very easy-going and was content to let him make the decisions about their planned activities, while remaining a thoroughly independent woman. The more he saw of her, the more he felt this was a seriously good thing. He began confiding in her, a few details about the rescue plan, also about being increasingly frustrated by the constraints of his volatile marriage. He was happy that he hadn't got Linda and her finances sorted out just yet. It gave him endless innocent excuses to keep flying to Perth. Mind you, he had better keep his mind on the job of sorting out Linda because if he wasn't careful, it could spell some nasty trouble. If he *was* careful, it would mean a bonus for him as well, one that Felicity would never have to know about. That would be a tidy nest egg to have waiting here for him if or when he got out of that mess back east. Felicity was a total pain to work with and there wasn't much let up when they weren't working. She was hard going all the time.

The mobile phone buzzing on the bedside table caused Gordon's good humour to dissipate. He picked it up and frowned, seeing it was his sister. Linda's agitated screech came staccato through: 'Oh God, *what have you done*, Gordie? What the hell have you done?'

'Christ, Linda. What are you on about? Cut the crap and speak sensibly, for heaven's sake! It can't be so hard to speak without the drama.' He spoke harshly, hoping to dampen her apparent near hysteria.

'Oh, Gordie, I just got the most awful fright. The police phoned looking for you!' She omitted explaining where the police rang from. 'They wouldn't say what they wanted. I told them you were at the Crowne. I just wanted to warn you. You haven't done something stupid, have you? I don't want any trouble.'

'Stop fussing. I told you not to worry. I've got it all under control. I could've done with a lot less of your customary histrionics. I'll call you back after they've rung.' He threw the phone on the bedside table.

He glanced down to see Antonia's green eyes focused on him and he bent to give her a quick kiss before standing up. He strode into the ensuite and rinsed his face with cold water to clear his head. His sense of well-being was well and truly banished. He had previously thought the yellow-tiled floor pattern in the ensuite was tasteful, now it simply irritated him.

'My sister just phoned to say the police are trying to get in touch with me. She said I was here. I'll take the call in the lounge, less disturbing for you.' He casually stroked a hand over her forehead.

As soon as she heard him answer the phone in the lounge, Antonia grabbed her phone and quickly texted: *Are things moving already? The cops have just rung Gordon.*

The reply was immediate: *Nothing to do with me! You'd better stay quiet, ears open to be on the safe side.*

Gordon's shoulders tensed when the caller identified himself as a policeman from New South Wales.

'Am I speaking to Gordon Hathaway?'

'Speaking.' He settled into the soft armchair.

'I'm afraid I have some rather bad news for you, sir.'

Gordon's stomach lurched. What was going on?

'Is your wife Felicity Hathaway?'

'She is,' Gordon replied, his brain suddenly racing.

'I'm afraid she was found deceased this morning and the death is being treated as suspicious,' the disembodied voice said in stiff police jargon.

The tension shot up behind Gordon's ribs like a steel punch. He jerked upright in his chair.

'What happened?' It was an effort to keep his voice steady and his hands still.

'It seems your stud manager found her in the stables this morning. We'd like you to return from Perth as soon as possible to help us with our enquiries.'

'But, what, how was she killed?'

'Ah, there was, um, a pitchfork, ah, in her back, sir. I'm sorry.'

'Oh, God,' Gordon felt the blood run from his face. He hadn't expected this. His breathing was fast and shallow. 'Oh, God.'

'What assistance can we give you in returning east, Sir?'

'None, none. I, ah, I have an open return ticket. Just have to ring the airline.' He stood up. 'I'll call them now if that's all you can tell me.'

'Please call us, sir, if there is anything we can do to help. Please accept our condolences.' The police officer relayed the number.

'Yes, yes. Thank you.' Gordon dropped the phone back

in place. He rubbed his hands over his face and dragged his fingers across his scalp. Antonia opened the bedroom door. She took in his strained face and crossed quickly to him.

'What is it?' Her voice was soft, and she stroked his shoulder.

When he mumbled out the few sparse details he had, Antonia's jaw dropped. The news was completely unexpected, hard to digest.

'I have to go back east straight away. I'm sorry,' he said in a low voice.

Antonia quickly gathered her wits and assumed a more appropriate expression: concern mixed with sympathy.

'Dear Gordon, don't be sorry. Of course, you must go back at once. What can I do to help?' It was surprisingly easy for her to sound genuinely concerned but harder to mask the relief that she felt knowing he was leaving so soon.

CHAPTER SIX

Ali Hadji sat hunched in the departure lounge of Sydney's international airport, scowling at his phone, chewing his fingernails. His head was reeling, and the leftover fumes of last night's vodka binge didn't help. *What haven't I taken care of?* kept playing over and over in his brain. He was sure he had forgotten to do something. *Why did it have to be last night that I decided to go on a binge?* He knew the answer: he was stressed from work. Mrs Hathaway had been bitchy and abrupt with him about the schedule for breaking the horses, contradicting what Mr Hathaway had told him before going to Perth. On top of that he was late with the repayments on the loan he'd taken earlier in the year to tide him over when he was short. When he was stressed, he longed for the comfort of his loving family back home in Syria. The late-night phone call had electrified him to action, cruelly cutting through the alcohol fog. He'd made a frantic search for his passport and booked himself on the cheapest and soonest available flight. He threw an assortment of clothes and a toiletry bag into a soft travel bag. Then, knowing he was too drunk to drive, he'd called a taxi to take him to Muswellbrook. By a stroke of good luck he was in time to catch the train to

Sydney. Now, sitting on the hard airport seats, he checked his watch for the hundredth time, scarcely believing he was going to make it on the flight. Food would make him feel better, he knew, but he worried he might be sick. He settled on a coffee, finishing it just as his flight was called. He threw the cup in the bin and almost ran to the boarding gate.

At Croham farm, the dust from the departing police vehicle had barely had time to settle before Gisella was back in full storm. She rounded on Silvio angrily.

'Why you not talk straight to police? They think you have something to hide when you go all dumb mouth. You got nothing to hide, my son? Where were you last night?' she yelled.

'Mama,' Silvio spread his hands wide in a calming gesture, 'You got nothing to worry about. I didn't kill Mrs Hathaway. How could you even think that of your own son?' He hoped to divert her by appealing to the maternal spirit. It had worked before, but he wasn't sure it would this time. Unfortunately, both his mother and his father had become seriously uneasy when the police arrived.

Burt's voice rumbled over Gisella's rapid fire reproaches. 'Where was ya, if ya got nothing to hide, Silvio? This is a serious business.'

'Dad, I was with a girl.' Before Silvio could add anything further, his mother immediately changed from nervously furious to cooing with excitement.

'Oh, Caro, a girl! Who is she? Why you keep her a secret? We so happy for you, aren't we Papa? Tell me all!'

Burt frowned when Silvio hesitated, wondering if the

"girl" was a convenient fabrication to put his parents off their questions. Gisella gave Silvio no time to reply, ecstatically giving rein to all her romantic hopes for her son, repeatedly imploring him to name the girl. She conveniently forgot she and Maria in Cessnock had plans to match Silvio with Maria's daughter. Silvio thought rapidly, trying to come up with a plausible name. Burt added his heavy, impatient voice to Gisella's, stressing the importance of allaying the possible suspicions of the police.

Silvio's brain froze. He felt cornered. 'It's Susannah!' he blurted.

Silence fell so swiftly that Silvio would have laughed if the situation had been less difficult. He turned rapidly away from his stunned parents, taking out his phone to text Susannah that he had revealed their relationship to them. He knew his parents would be against the relationship. *Do I want it to continue, or was it a pleasant fling?* He felt confused, knowing that if he *was* serious about Susannah, he would have to be there to support her through her mother's death, as well as dealing with his parent's disapproval. *How would her father handle it?* He wondered if he had the commitment or the maturity to cope with all that.

* * *

Jarred Green walked down the length of the stables checking the work the lads had completed. He felt an added weight of responsibility to keep things running smoothly until Mr Hathaway returned from Perth. He was keen not to give any reason to be asked to find another job. He frowned when he realised the lunging yard was empty and quiet. *Where the hell is that Ali Hadji?* Jarred strode down to the tack shed, calling loudly, 'Has anyone seen Ali this morning?'

No one had seen him. Jarred used his mobile and tried to call Ali. The phone went to voice mail, so he left a message for Ali to call him immediately. He scrolled through his contacts and selected a number, pressing 'call'.

'Jack Dawson speaking.'

'Jack. Jarred Green here from Divine Hayfields.'

'Hey Jarred, how're ya goin?'

'Jack, I hate to bother you, but I know you live next door to my trainer, Ali Hadji and I wonder if you've seen him this morning?' Jarred tried to speak casually to avoid raising any awkward questions.

'Ahh, let's see,' Jack drawled. 'I left home about quarter to eight and his car was still in his driveway, but I haven't actually seen him since the weekend. You got a problem?'

'Nah, Jack, not really. He just hasn't turned up here yet. But not to worry, thanks. I'll try a few others, but if you see him, can you let him know I'm looking for him, please?'

'Sure will, mate,' Jack responded and hung up.

He didn't want to call the police for what may be a minor glitch but Jarred had to face the fact that someone had been murdered and someone else was missing. Whichever way you looked at it, it was not good news. He sighed, reluctantly reached into his pocket, and dragged out the business card the police had left.

'Wharton speaking,' Ben answered.

'Jarred Green here.' He hesitated a second, then said, 'I guess you should know; the horse trainer hasn't turned up at work today. His car is still at his house, according to a neighbour, but nobody has seen him around.'

Ben felt his interest spike but kept his voice calm while quickly flipping through his notes, 'What's his name again? Oh yes, here it is Ali Hadji. Is that right?'

'Yeah, that's him,' Jarred confirmed.

'Okay, Jarred, I'll need you to give me his phone number and address.'

'I tried his mobile, but it went to voicemail,' Jarred said. He then read out Ali's number from the digital display on his phone and supplied the address in Wheeler.

'Well, that's interesting,' Ben said. 'Is he usually reliable? Got any friends he might have stayed with last night? A girlfriend? Does he drink, do you know?'

'No, I don't think he drinks too much. He sometimes joins us in the pub on Saturday night, but I've never seen him especially drunk. I don't know any of his friends, girls or fellers.'

'We'll check it out and I'll get back to you. Thanks for letting us know, Jarred. Nothing else has cropped up out there, has it?'

'No, we're just carrying on with what we can. Have you been in touch with Mr Hathaway?' Jarred felt that the sooner the boss was back in control, the better.

'Yeah, we got onto him and he's getting a flight back today. You should see him back at Divine Hayfields tomorrow, I'd think,' Ben said.

'That's a relief.' Jarred thoughtfully cut the connection

from his call to the detective.

At that moment, Ali Hadji felt the thump as the wheels of the A380 retracted into the body of the aircraft. He looked out the window at the view of Botany Bay while the plane banked round to its course for the Middle East. He heaved a trembling sigh of relief knowing at last that he was definitely on his way.

Jarred walked to the feed shed to see how work was progressing. He looked in the doorway and found Jason, the mechanic had caught his usual ride with Mrs Sullivan. He was fully absorbed in catching up on all the details of the night's tragedy, listening avidly as the lads supplied as much detail as they knew and invented what they didn't know. Despite the slight relief that Jason had turned up for work, Jarred was irritated that they were so irresponsibly wasting time.

'Hey, look, guys! You've all got better things to do than sit around gossiping like a bunch of breathless schoolgirls. Whatever has happened, it's not our business to discuss it. There's work to be done here. Mr Hathaway will probably be back tomorrow, and I don't want him thinking we're not up to the task of keeping things going when he's not here. With Mrs Hathaway's death he may be spending time away with the police and solicitors and so on and he needs to know everything will carry on without him. I know it's upsetting, and our routine is shot but how about we all crack on with our jobs.' Jarred didn't like rebuking the lads, but he liked even less the fact that they so readily forgot their responsibilities to indulge in a ghoulish recap of events. 'What did you have scheduled today, Jason?' Jarred asked.

'I was supposed to be getting the mulcher ready to go over the two yearling paddocks up the top,' Jason responded.

'Well, you get on with that,' Jarred said, 'and when you're done, I want you to check and service all the farm vehicles, including checking the tyres. The rest of you had better carry on with your work or you'll be late finishing tonight.' He turned away from the doorway, then heard his name called.

Hamish hurried out of the feed shed with an anxious look on his face.

'What is it, Hamish?' Jarred asked, not unkindly.

'I'm frightened. There'sakillerhere. I don'twanttodie. I can't stay here!' In his panic, Hamish tumbled his words out so fast they all ran together. His face was white, and his bottom lip trembled.

Jarred's heart sank. The last thing he wanted to deal with was a case of hysterics. He thought fast: *should I try to calm Hamish down, reassuring him, or should I let him go?* The near future looked pretty complicated already; *do I want to add to my problems by keeping on a worker who looks as if he is going to be needing constant reassurance?* Jarred tried to weigh up the best option: short-handed by letting Hamish go, or having time taken up each day keeping Hamish on a steady keel? He thought he knew what his decision would be but he'd at least give Hamish a chance to say his piece.

'Look, what exactly is worrying you?' he asked, trying to sound kind and patient at the same time.

'Ali did an axe-throwing course in Sydney!' Hamish blurted out, 'He was telling us about it. He really enjoyed it. He reckoned it'd surprise you how far you can throw an axe.'

'What? When was this?' Jarred felt his heart lurch. He tried to quell the feeling of horror that took a hold of him.

'He was telling us about it last week. What if he used the stuff he'd learnt to jab Mrs Hathaway with the pitchfork?' Hamish gagged as the image of the murdered woman crowded his mind.

'Let's not jump to conclusions here, Hamish. I don't think it's the same thing, throwing an axe and throwing a pitchfork, but I'll tell the police.' Jarred thought quickly, trying to sort out the best course of action. 'I'm glad you told me, but I think you're worrying over nothing.' He paused while he made his decision. 'Look, if you're not comfortable here, there's no point in staying, even though you will be leaving me short a man. I'll give you a decent reference and Darren can make up your final pay to forward on to you if you like. Don't change your phone number. We have to know where to find you so we can get your pay to you but also in case the police want to talk to you further.' Jarred looked at Hamish and realised he was close to tears.

'Will the police really want to talk to me? I don't know anything!' There was a quiver in his voice.

'Of course, mate,' Jarred said patiently, 'you know they have to make all their enquiries. That little bit of information you just shared could very well help them get a clearer picture of what went on. I'm pretty sure they'll want to ask everyone more questions. Don't worry about it if you've nothing to hide. Just make sure I can contact you if necessary. You're no use here if you can't work. Do you really want to go?'

Hamish eagerly nodded his head. 'I don't like it here anymore.'

'Well, go and pack your things. I'll talk to Darren and get that reference written. Hamish, you're a good worker. You should try to be a bit more confident and believe in yourself.'

Hamish looked at Jarred. 'Really?' he said.

'Yeah, mate. If you showed more confidence in yourself, the others would ease up on you.' Jarred regretted that he hadn't taken more time to bolster Hamish's confidence, but he was a manager not a nursemaid.

'Take it easy and don't worry. Just try to be more assertive at your new job. If I hear of anyone wanting staff, I'll let you know.'

'Thanks for that. Bye, then.'

'Be seeing you, Hamish. Good luck.'

Hamish turned and headed disconsolately towards the cottage.

Jarred shook his head in resignation, realising he had made the right choice not trying to talk Hamish into staying, even though it meant more work for the rest of the lads. He thought about Hamish's revelation and wondered whether axe-throwing and pitchfork-throwing were the same, despite his reassurances to Hamish. He shuddered. Then it occurred to him he probably didn't even have Ali Hadji to fill in any staffing gaps. *Damn!*

Ben Wharton disconnected from Jarred. He walked to Kaylee's desk and shared the gist of the call. He was interrupted by Kaylee's phone ringing. She held up a finger to Ben, answering the call. As she listened, her eyebrows rose. After a few questions regarding times, she thanked the caller and hung up.

'This is getting interesting, Ben. That was Police Help Line. They have received an anonymous call regarding Mrs Hathaway's death. And this call is pointing the finger guess where?'

'No idea,' Ben said.

'The caller said we should interview Vicar Aligardy at the church in Wheeler as he would be sure to have helpful information. What do you make of that?'

'Really?' Ben found it hard to believe that a man of religion could be involved in a murder, but then he reasoned, the vicar may not necessarily be involved, just might know something. 'Looks like we hit the road again,' he said. 'We have to find the axe-throwing horse trainer. And now we must interview the vicar, too. Wheeler, here we come. That is, if you're free to leave your desk,' he added with semi-mock deference to Kaylee. She grinned, standing up and said, 'Lead on.'

Soon they were back in Wheeler, pulling up in front of the attractive old church. The greying bricks were covered with moss where shade from a massive oak tree on the south facing wall kept it damp and cool. They parked on a small gravel area and walked between the church and the weatherboard hall to a rusty gate at the back. The path led them to the side door of a modest brick cottage that was obviously from more modern times than the church.

Kaylee knocked and they both stepped back to wait for an answer.

CHAPTER SEVEN

A solidly built greying man of middle height opened the door with a welcoming smile on his face.

'What can I do to help?' he asked genially.

'Detective Sergeant Kaylee Bradshaw, and this is Detective Senior Constable Ben Wharton,' she said.

'Are you Vicar Aligardy?' He nodded. 'We'd like to have a word with you if you have a moment.'

Vicar Aligardy stepped aside from the door and gestured for the two detectives to follow him inside. They walked down a short hallway that opened into an airy light kitchen with backyard views from the two windows. The vicar indicated the kitchen chairs round the table with a sweep of his arm. 'Sit.'

Once they were all seated, the vicar steepled his hands in front of his chest and raised his eyebrows enquiringly. Ben was struck by the overall calm in the man and the economy of movement that gave him an air of stillness from within.

Kaylee said, 'We were called to Divine Hayfields this morning. We're currently gathering information which could lead us to some conclusions in our enquiries. Are Mr and Mrs Hathaway known to you?' Her sharp eyes noted a tightening in the vicar's jaw, but he remained composed.

'Yes, I know them both. They are members of my congregation.'

'And how would you describe your relationship with them?'

'I like Mr Hathaway a lot. He is a man of decisive actions and intelligent opinions. He has a well-formed idea of what is of overall benefit to this community, and he is willing to help work towards those benefits.'

'What about Mrs Hathaway?' Ben suggested when the vicar paused.

'Ah well, she is an entirely different individual! She is no less committed to the good of the community than her husband, but she feels that *her* way is the best way of doing things. She likes her own way, to put it bluntly.'

'You're speaking from experience, are you?' Kaylee asked.

'Oh yes.' Some of the vicar's inner stillness dissolved as he recalled the last meeting of the community building committee. 'Mrs Hathaway seems to think that because I am a man of God, I have no individual identity and am therefore a pushover,' the vicar said decisively. 'But I, too, know what is good for my community and I also know how to work with the community to achieve those ends. I happen to know that communities appreciate the things they have *jointly* worked to achieve. Mrs Hathaway, on the other hand, thinks that throwing money towards projects in a grand gesture will not only get things done but will also generate the undying gratitude of the community.'

'What exactly is this project, Vicar?' Ben asked.

'Through a community building initiative, we applied

for and were awarded a grant towards improving our sport facilities that would enable us to cater to a wider cross-section of the local population. By "a wider cross-section", I, and a number of others on the committee, understood it to mean children, teens and adults. We don't want just a skate park, for example, as that has a limited range of appeal. We had in mind some courts marked out for basketball, tennis and netball, games all age groups can play. And we thought maybe a putt-putt golf course for the little children. We have been given a vacant block next to my church hall, so we can open the hall for catering at events in the sport facilities. The grant is not sufficient to achieve our design, so we decided to raise the balance through fundraisers. Mrs Hathaway just wants to play Lady Bountiful, donate the balance of the funds and have a huge plaque of grateful thanks erected to her. Of course, this has raised hackles among the locals, none of whom like being runover roughshod. They might not all be as wealthy or as well educated as Mrs Hathaway, but nevertheless this is their community as well as hers and they deserve to have their opinions acknowledged and respected. They have their pride. There have been some very fierce discussions.' The vicar's voice was rising, and he scowled, recollecting his last frustrating encounter with Felicity.

'How about you, personally, have you had words with Mrs Hathaway?' Ben questioned.

'Of course I have!' the vicar said forcefully. Her attitude at the last committee meeting was still fresh in his memory. She had really needled him, testing his patience well and truly. 'She doesn't suffer fools gladly and neither do I! I *know* this community. I know what she wants to do *won't* work. I can't make her see reason! She is very trying, and I don't envy Gordon and the effort he must make daily to maintain the peace. Sorry. This is a topic that I feel strongly about because I know that if we do it properly, we can make a really positive improvement for a large number of community members. It'll help raise morale when everyone can gather together and share good times as well as hard times. It'll be a great venue for people to get to know each other. It'll give kids a place to gather and burn off steam safely. It'll really help knit everyone together and that can only be a good thing.' Vicar Aligardy paused and collected himself. He realised he'd allowed his excitement to run away and then added more moderately, 'Was there something specific you wanted to know?'

'Where were you last night?'

'Last night, I visited the Morris family next door to the school and stayed for dinner. Why do you ask?'

'I think it fair to tell you, that we were called to Divine Hayfields this morning because Mrs Hathaway has been killed,' Ben's voice was gentle.

'Killed? Goodness me! That is a terrible thing. How is Gordon coping?' The vicar bowed his head making the sign of the cross, his lips moving in silent prayer.

'Gordon is in Perth.'

'You can't think I would be involved in that! Sure, she threatened to go over my head to get me to agree to her donation proposal but come on, that's not grounds for murder. Mind you she could have made my life difficult if she *had* gone over my head. I am happy here and not keen to see it end any time soon. Anyone passing could have seen my car at the Morris' all evening. I came home about half past eight.'

'Well thank you for your help. Oh, do you know the Hathaway's horse trainer, Ali Hadji?' Ben asked.

'I know of him, but I don't know him. He's not a member of my parish.'

'Okay, Vicar. Thanks again for your help. Please call if you think of anything you've forgotten to tell us,' Kaylee said, pushing her card across the table.

Vicar Aligardy thoughtfully watched the police walk away down the path. He wondered if he could have handled that interview any better. He knew he still tended to get very intense over issues close to his heart. Years of practising strict self-control could be unravelled in a moment, much to his regret. He had allowed himself to be unsettled by Mrs Hathaway the other night, especially when she started the finger jabbing and the threatening. But he'd put it out of his mind once he calmed down. *Who would have told the police to look at me? Or are they interviewing the whole village?* He thought everyone else had left the building after the meeting when she was giving him a piece of her mind. He didn't think anyone else knew.

The police drove the short distance to Ali Hadji's house. They knocked but had no response. Ben walked round the side of the building, peering through the windows. From what he could see, it looked as if someone had ransacked the place but maybe Ali just kept a messy home. Ben tried the back door which was locked. He went back to where Kaylee was waiting and shared his findings.

'Do we get a search warrant?' Ben asked.

'I guess we have to,' Kaylee sighed, thinking of the paperwork. 'The man is missing. We're dealing with a murder. Best not to leave any stones unturned. We'll just ask at the store if they have seen him.'

CHAPTER EIGHT

lthough the store was centrally situated and had a clear view of most of the village, the owner hadn't seen Ali. He volunteered the name and address of the people who rented their house to Ali but otherwise he couldn't help. While Kaylee spoke to the store owner, Ben stepped over to the bakery and ordered a couple of sandwiches. He took two iced coffees from the fridge display and paid. Back at the store, Kaylee stood to one side, talking to the office about the search warrant. Ben casually read the noticeboard while waiting, noting that an event was planned at the church hall that weekend, raising funds for the sporting facilities. They walked out into the empty street, leant on their car while they ate.

'I'd like to go back up to the stud to talk to a few people a bit more before Mr Hathaway gets back. His presence might have a damping effect on people's willingness to share,' Ben said with a wry smile around a mouthful.

'Who are you interested in?' Kaylee was curious, trying to follow his thought process.

'These are the people who I think were less than forthcoming with us before: Darren, Susannah, Silvio, Kevin Craig, possibly Burt. We didn't even talk to the housekeeper or the mechanic or the casual guy who comes up with Mrs Sullivan or the one from the village, what was his name? Mac? What did you think of the vicar?' Ben responded.

'He certainly didn't seem to have got on with Mrs Hathaway, but he seemed straightforward about it. I didn't get the feeling he was hiding any guilty secrets, did you?'

'Nah, it was just wishful thinking that we could add yet another suspect to our huge list!' Ben said. 'We have plenty of people with a grievance against Mrs Hathaway and plenty of people who could have killed her. I still have misgivings about that pitchfork being the cause of death, though. It just seems all wrong to me,' he added.

'Clicks and Paul should have something definitive by tomorrow, I'd think. We got lucky with the coroner. They're not run off their feet in Newcastle and said they could send someone up to do the job this afternoon. So, we'll have plenty of info to sift through in the morning,' Kaylee said confidently.

She threw her lunch rubbish in the bin on the kerb and said 'Coming?'

Ben climbed in and they drove back up the dusty road to Divine Hayfields.

Ben nodded his head towards the church. 'I see there is a fundraiser at the church hall this weekend.'

'Really? What's on?'

'A night market, food stalls, music, dancing, games for the kids. Sounds pretty comprehensive,' Ben said.

'Maybe we should go,' Kaylee said thoughtfully. Her mind quickly skipped to a more pressing idea. 'If we see

Silvio by himself anywhere along here, we'll stop and question him. We won't get anything out of him with his parents around.'

Paddocks with new spring growth and neat fences dotted with contentedly grazing cattle and horses flashed past. The ornate gates to Croham had just disappeared behind them when Kaylee spotted a dirt bike on the road ahead of them.

'Could be Silvio, Ben,' she said. 'Let's catch him before he gets to Divine Hayfields.'

They deftly caught up and passed the rider, pulling him over. It *was* Silvio as Kaylee had hoped and he showed some frustration at being pulled over.

'What do you want now?' he asked impatiently.

'I don't think you were quite honest with us about your whereabouts last night,' Kaylee said cheerfully.

'I told you I was with Susannah,' he responded shortly.

Ben cut in forcefully, 'Susannah! You just said "a girl", not Susannah Hathaway! Don't be wasting our time, mate. Remember, we're investigating a murder. If you can't satisfy us about where you've been and what you've been up to then we'll have to take you into the station.'

As he'd hoped, his words edged Silvio towards being a little more cooperative.

'Zanna and I can't meet at her place. Her mother was pretty strict, and anyway we hadn't told anyone about our relationship,' he said.

'Why was that?' Kaylee asked.

'You must have noticed my dad is not exactly flavour of the month with the Hathaways. We couldn't see either of our parents being rapt that we were together. My old-fashioned and sometimes over-the-top Italian mother has her eye on the daughter of a friend of hers in Cessnock for me. Of all the stupid ideas! It just wasn't worth the hassle to tell them.'

'So, where were you?' Ben pressed.

'The farm next door to Dad's belongs to a guy who lives at his other property east of Denman. We spend a lot of time on the back veranda there in the evenings, private, undisturbed. We met up there about half-seven last night. Spent a couple of hours relaxing. I think I got home about ten, maybe a little later.'

'Romantic,' murmured Kaylee ironically, 'So how did you get there?'

'It's about fifteen minutes' walk from home. I walked up and met Zanna there. She drove up in her car and then she dropped me at my gate on her way home.'

'Were you on your way to see Susannah just now?' Ben asked. 'If you were, we'll follow you up there. But please help us out by not texting or calling her before we can talk to her. You want her to be able to back up your story, don't you?'

'Yeah, I guess,' Silvio nodded. He resented the police presence but suddenly realised how awful the situation must be for Susannah. He felt a rush of protectiveness for her.

'I'll follow you up,' he murmured.

Hearing the vehicles, Susannah came out onto the veranda when they arrived. She ran lightly down to Silvio and embraced him, drawing comfort and strength from his embrace.

'Zanna,' he said with a note of warning, 'The police want to ask you a few more questions. Answer them. I'll stay with you.'

He felt her body droop, and he squeezed her shoulders reassuringly. He was glad when he felt her stiffen and pull herself together. *I'm still not sure I'm ready to deal with a crying girlfriend yet,* he thought.

She stood aside from him and faced the police, 'Well?'

'When was the last time you saw your mum, Susannah?' Kaylee asked gently.

'Dar and I had dinner with Mum about half-past-six. She was talking to Jarred before that.' Susannah spoke in a restrained voice, showing little emotion. 'We just had a grill and salad. Mum and I had a glass of wine. Dar had water; he doesn't drink much. Silvio and I had agreed to meet later. I had a shower and left about ten or quarter past seven. I called to her I'd be out for a while and waved. She was still at the kitchen bench, had a fresh glass of wine in front of her. She waved.' Susannah's voice broke as she realised how mundane her last exchange with her mother had been. She straightened her back. It was not in her nature to cave in and cry. She was really missing her mum, despite their rocky relationship. Her mum was, after all, a woman, and she could always tell when Susannah needed a hug. *Silvio will have to hurry up and get to know me well enough to know when I need a hug.*

'So, where did you go?' Ben prodded.

Susannah glanced at Silvio and he nodded reassuringly. She blushed. 'I met Sil up at Thompson's place. Mr Thompson doesn't live there and it's a quiet place we can be without the parents hassling us. We were there a couple of hours. Then I dropped him off and went home.' Kaylee nodded with satisfaction and said, 'Did you see your mum when you got home?'

'No,' Susannah's voice wavered a bit, 'I just went to my room. The front light was on, but I don't think the kitchen one was. I wasn't sure who was in and who wasn't, so I left the lights as they were.' Always aware of her budget and her expenditure, the careful Kaylee mentally gasped at the casual waste of electricity but kept her face impassive.

'And you stayed in your room for the night?'

'Yes, until you came up. Did you get in touch with dad?'

'He should be home sometime tomorrow, I think,' Ben said. Then he added, 'Okay, well you two can go about your business for now, but could you call Darren, please.'

The two detectives sat on the veranda taking in the view and waiting for Darren.

'Actually, Ben, how about you talk to Mrs Sullivan while I talk to Darren? Could save us a bit of time and I'm sure I can handle Darren,' Kaylee suggested.

Ben nodded and wandered towards the kitchen.

He found Mrs Sullivan in the laundry and introduced himself. Her attitude was brisk and no-nonsense. She expressed surprise and distaste at the news of Mrs Hathaway's death but no obvious sorrow. After a short chat, he had found out nothing new. Mrs Sullivan was respectful of her employers, but not, apparently, attached to them. When Ben asked her about Jason, she said she didn't think much of him, but Ben gathered that was mostly because of his irresponsible approach to driving. She added that he paid her for petrol and had changed a tyre for her once when she had a flat, so she tolerated him. Hearing Kaylee and Darren talking on the veranda, Ben thanked Mrs Sullivan and left the house by the back door. He headed towards the stables in search of Kevin Craig.

'Darren,' Kaylee said, 'how are you holding up? We got onto your dad and he should be back here tomorrow sometime. Can you answer a few more questions for me?'

She didn't give him time to reply and went on, 'What did you do yesterday evening?'

Darren's head jerked up. 'Nothing!'

'Darren, you're not doing yourself any favours by keeping things back. Help me out here,' Kaylee urged.

'I just went for a walk after dinner,' He frowned slightly, knowing how lame it sounded.

'Where? Who did you see? How long were you out? What are you avoiding telling me?' Kaylee decided a little more pressure might get Darren to open up.

'I, I ...' Darren wondered how much to say.

'Look, Darren, we're talking about your mother's murder here. Did you kill your mother?' Kaylee was suddenly impatient to make some progress.

'NO! No, I didn't! I couldn't. How could you think that I could?'

'Well, you're not being very helpful, are you. Now tell me what you did last evening.'

'Ok. Sorry,' he made an effort to sound cooperative. 'Dinner was pretty uncomfortable. Mum and Zanna were at each other's throats. Mum knew Zanna was seeing someone and she wanted to know who it was. She takes advantage of Dad being away to question her. Dad always stands up for Susannah and makes mum back off.'

'Why didn't Susannah want your mother to know about Silvio?' Darren's head snapped up. 'Yes, Darren, we know about Silvio. So why the big secret?'

'Come on, even without knowing mum in person, you must realise that the son of the Bunracks would not be acceptable to her! Mum is ... *was*, very socially aware and the Bunracks didn't come close to the bottom rung of my mother's ladder,' Ben said forcefully.

'Ok, so, after your frosty meal together, what did you do?' Kaylee figured if she kept forcing, Darren might tell her.

'Oh, I just felt restless. I didn't feel like going into town for a drink, but I didn't want to stay in the house. I went down to the creek and wandered along the banks for a while, but it got cool out, so I came home.'

Kaylee thought she hadn't heard anything quite so unconvincing in a long time. 'Did you see anyone? Did you stop in at the lad's cottage?'

'No!' Darren's face reddened. 'I told you, I just walked along the creek.'

'What time did you get back to the house? Did you see your mother?' Kaylee tried a different tack.

'My bedroom is on the veranda side of the house and has a French door. I didn't come in past the kitchen. I didn't see mum,' he gulped a bit. 'I didn't even say goodbye or anything, you know.' He dropped his head into his hands and sighed deeply. 'What a mess,' he said, almost to himself.

Kaylee regarded his bowed head thoughtfully. 'I still think there's more you could tell me,' she said seriously.

'So, you just call me when you're ready to start talking. I know it's not easy for you, but I'm sure you want to give us all the help you can, to find out who killed your mother.'

She left Darren and went out to the car where she made some notes while she waited for Ben.

At the stable complex, Ben saw Jarred and waved a greeting.

'Where can I find Kevin?' he asked.

Jarred gestured towards the back of the stables. 'He's in the exercise ring with Divine Madam.'

'Do you mind if I ask him a few questions?' Ben had decided that he would guarantee maximum cooperation from everyone by keeping all his interactions very polite.

'Sure, you do what you have to do. The sooner this mess is cleared up the better. You got onto Mr Hathaway, didn't you?'

'Yes,' Ben replied. 'He should be back tomorrow.'

'Oh right, I forgot. There's a bit much going on.'

Jarred had become more and more anxious as the day wore on, otherwise he would have remembered Ben had told him when Mr Hathaway would be back. He was relieved that he could soon share some of the responsibilities. He didn't doubt his ability to keep things running properly in the absence of his bosses but Mrs Hathaway's death, *murder*, had left him feeling very uneasy. *Who is the murderer?* Jarred couldn't get his head round the idea that someone right here on Divine Hayfields was a killer. *But it had to be someone from here!* Common sense told him the involvement of an outsider was very unlikely. He didn't like the fact that since his discovery of Mrs Hathaway this morning, he looked at everyone differently, suspiciously. He felt jumpy and inclined to imagine the worst reasons for everyone's actions. He found himself watching the lads more closely as they worked. He was also troubled by the absence of Ali. He had liked the guy, trusted him, admired his work. *Where has he got to?* Jarred worried. He had thought he was a good judge of men and now he was not so sure. *Have I been wrong about Ali?* He had also thought Hamish had more backbone than he had shown by clearing-off at the first hint of trouble. *Who else have I been wrong about?* Admittedly, he didn't have the final say when it came to hiring and firing staff, but both Mr and Mrs Hathaway had made no secret of the fact that they trusted Jarred's judgement. For the first time since beginning work at Divine Hayfields, Jarred felt the load of his responsibilities very heavily. *Did I miss something last night? Was someone behaving oddly yesterday, and I didn't notice? The only person behaving differently was Mrs Hathaway herself, and really, she was only being more capricious and hard to please than usual.* With an anxious frown, he watched Ben leave the stables.

Ben strolled over to the exercise ring where Kevin was trotting the mare round on a long, light rein. She was satiny black, groomed flawlessly. She clearly enjoyed her exercise as she trotted round with her ears pricked alertly forward and her head held up. As soon as she saw Ben, her head swung towards him. This drew Kevin's attention to his arrival, and he turned frowning.

'Hi, Kevin. Have you got a few minutes to spare?' Ben called in a steady voice. 'Jarred said I'd find you here. You've got the mare looking stunning, I must say.'

Kevin didn't welcome the interruption to his program, but he appreciated Ben's recognition of his work with the mare. He allowed her to slow to a walk and led her over to the tall wooden fence of the exercise ring. Ben stretched his hand to the mare's nose, letting her snuffle his fingers before gently smoothing his hand down her shiny neck.

'I didn't get a chance to ask this morning, but did you see anyone while you were walking yesterday evening?' Ben thought he may as well jump straight in.

'No,' Kevin's voice was curt.

'Why walk? I'd have thought you got enough exercise while you worked?'

'It helps me clear my head.'

'How long were you walking?'

'About an hour. I got back in time to clean up for dinner.'

'Did you notice anyone acting strangely yesterday? Anyone under particular strain? Kevin, I get the feeling you are not willing to be talking to me, but you must understand that this is a murder enquiry. It can be nothing else. Mrs Hathaway didn't throw a pitchfork into her own back!'

'Okay! Look, this isn't an easy place to work. On any given day, someone is feeling stressed. With Mr Hathaway going backwards and forwards from Perth, there was never any continuity. He'd talk to Jarred and leave us with directions about carrying on while he was away and then when he left, she'd give us new directions. When you can see what makes sense and what doesn't, it's frustrating having to cope with the continual changes of plans. We all know what our job is. Jarred is a good manager. It'd be a lot easier if we could just get on with things.'

Ben was encouraged that Kevin suddenly seemed more compliant, so he pressed on. 'How long have you been working here? If it's so frustrating, why do you stay? How long has Mr Hathaway been going backwards and forwards, as you put it? How long is he usually away?'

'The job is the horses,' Kevin said simply. 'I love them. I've been here about five years, pays good. Even though there are constantly changing orders, basically I'm working with horses whatever the orders are. I think Mr Hathaway started going to Perth about eight or nine months ago, maybe more. He's usually away about a week or ten days.' Kevin's hands started to sweat. Keeping track of everything he had said was getting more and more difficult. His stomach had been in knots for days with the strain of trying not to let out what he knew.

'Did you kill Mrs Hathaway?' Ben asked bluntly. He wasn't satisfied that Kevin's apparent honesty was genuine, so he decided to try to frighten an up-front response from him.

Kevin was shocked at the direct question. 'No! Absolutely not.'

Ben sighed in frustration. 'Ok, Kevin. I still think you can tell me more than you have, so feel free to call me any time.' He held out his card. 'Remember this is a murder we're investigating. We're not just going to go away.'

Kevin was all too aware they were not "just going to go away" but he wished it could have been that simple. He turned back to the mare and led her away to the centre of the ring, hoping to get some peace of mind working with the stately horse.

Ben walked back to the police vehicle. He felt discouraged and frustrated that he still sensed Kevin was keeping something back. He wondered how Kaylee fared with Darren.

Bumping over the unsealed road back to Wheeler, they agreed that both Kevin and Darren knew more than they were letting on.

Kaylee phoned the station and learnt that the search warrant of Ali's house had been issued, so they decided to defer any further questioning of Burt Bunrack in favour of spending time executing the warrant.

They picked up a key from Ali's landlord and drove to his cottage, a neat, white building with minimal gardens. Ben handed Kaylee gloves and they stood on the garden path as they donned the regulation equipment. Ben stepped up to the door, unlocking it and standing back for Kaylee to walk in.

'Let's see what went on here,' Kaylee said stepping inside. 'Phew, what a mess!'

The cottage was small with two bedrooms off the right of the entry hall and a lounge/dining room on the left. The kitchen and bathroom were at the back of the house. The air throughout had the stale smells of alcohol and food. Clothing was scattered on the floor in both bedrooms. Cupboard doors and drawers hung open. The bed in one room was a rumpled mess and the bed in the other was clearly unused. In the lounge room, the same disarray prevailed. The drawers of the desk were open revealing a mess of paperwork. Some papers had spilled onto the floor. An almost empty vodka bottle stood on the table beside a half full glass. The kitchen benches were cluttered with unwashed dishes. An empty foil container showed that Ali had eaten a frozen dinner-for-one at some stage. In the bathroom, although it was the least messy, the cabinet door was open. A damp towel lay on the floor and dirty work clothes were piled in the corner. There was no toothbrush or shaving gear to be seen.

Ben prowled through, careful not to disturb anything, frowning with concentration.

'I don't think there could have been a struggle, even though it's such a mess,' Kaylee said. 'Nothing is knocked over, not the bottle or the glass or any chairs. Nothing seems to be broken. There's no blood that I can see.'

'So, what happened?'

'I'd say, he came home and showered off the day's dirt by the look of the bathroom. Looks like he's had a drink, but hard to tell how much. How full was the bottle to start with? He has had a feed if you can call those frozen meals a feed. On his own at that stage ...' Kaylee thought about possible scenarios.

'I reckon he's left in a hurry. Why has he left? Maybe he packed. He was possibly hunting for clothes to pack. There are no toiletries in the bathroom. What was he looking for in the desk? Wait a minute! He's not Australian, is he? Maybe he was looking for his passport. Why? Quick exit on an international flight? Was he alone? Was someone forcing him?'

'I think we'd better get onto Immigration to see if he's left the country. I'll just ring the constable on the desk and ask him to get onto that now. We'll have to get Clicks and Paul to go through here tomorrow. There's not much of today left. Probably time we called it a day anyway. My head is full and fresh eyes in the morning could help.' Kaylee rubbed her forehead and stepped outside, peeling off her gloves. 'This has been one interesting day and I kind of doubt we'll be getting any answers tomorrow. Probably just more questions.' She smiled ruefully.

Ben double-checked the front door was locked and they drove back to the police station in thoughtful silence.

CHAPTER NINE

On the other side of Australia, Ms Antonia Larson walked confidently along St Georges Terrace. Her mood was upbeat since farewelling Gordon Hathaway at the airport that morning. It suited her well to have his visit cut short. She walked casually, enjoying the fresh air on her face. Her auburn curls bounced in a shiny mass as the light breeze caught them. She knew that her cream linen pant suit showed off her perfect figure and complimented her flawless olive skin. She turned left through a doorway and stepped down into the underground bar. The trademark smell of popcorn wafted through the cool dark room. She selected a table by the wall and relaxed into a leather upholstered easy chair to wait.

Antonia was looking forward to a little downtime this evening. Her work had been neglected while Gordon was there, and she had been happy to knuckle down to a hard day's work. She spent time working on several litigation cases that were demanding attention and attended two dispute resolution meetings. A glow of satisfaction enhanced the feeling of well-being brought on by the mild evening air.

Antonia had aimed high all her life. She realised early in her career that intelligence and an attractive personality were a winning combination, which she exploited to the full. She was recognised as a formidable lawyer in the business community of Perth, and she sat on several boards of directors. Ms Larson enjoyed her success, her money and her prestige and she was never quite sure which of those she enjoyed most.

In the dimly lit bar, Antonia didn't have long to wait for her companion. She recognised his long legs coming down the stairs and smiled a welcome. He met her eyes and pointed to the bar, eyebrows raised. When Antonia nodded, he stopped to order.

Logan Kirby looked every inch the wealthy man he was. Tall, slim, a few grey hairs flecked among his short dark hair. He was clean-shaven which made him look quite reliable rather than ruthless. Only on closer inspection did his brown eyes reveal a cold lack of compassion, although he cleverly diluted that impression by habitually appearing cheerfully good-natured. He carried the drinks to Antonia, putting them on the table before kissing her lightly on the cheek she offered.

He and Antonia had known each other from high school days. They had an easy, undemanding friendship, both knowing they had talents the other could use. They'd attended the same university, but Logan had completed his studies when he achieved his Master of Business Administration. He borrowed from an uncle to set up a construction company at the time that Perth was experiencing a building boom. He capitalised on every opportunity that offered and was not afraid to take risks where others stepped away. Logan quickly expanded his business to set up the Kirby Construction company and soon developed a varied portfolio of assets, including real estate and shares. At the same time, he grew a reputation for being a hard-headed, shrewd dealer, with a talent for making money where there seemed no likelihood of profiting. A few times, he had offered Antonia the opportunity to join his ventures and they'd both profited. They enjoyed each other's company and worked well together. Antonia prized Logan's ability to turn a little cash into a lot of cash. Logan valued having Antonia's legal connections in case he found himself in difficulties.

His latest investment direction was into the world of horse racing. He was immensely proud of his two racehorses and had every intention of acquiring more. He loved the thrilling sensation of being trackside as the huge, glossy creatures streamed past with their colourful cargo of jockeys. He was too canny to gamble large amounts but thoroughly enjoyed rubbing shoulders with the wealthy and well-connected in general and the greats of the racing world in particular.

Logan knew the importance of supporting the community and he made sure that his charitable work was well-known among his high-profile business associates. What he was careful to keep incredibly quiet were his occasional but very worthwhile ventures into some particularly shady businesses.

'Busy day?' she asked, raising her glass in a toast.

'Yeah,' he replied shortly, taking a swallow. 'So, what's going on? I haven't had time to set anything up yet. Got quite a surprise when you texted this morning that the cops were on their way.'

'It was very early. They came to tell Gordon that his wife had been killed,' Antonia updated him. Logan's eyebrows rose in surprise.

'Yes,' she murmured. 'Apparently its murder. Rather hard to make a pitchfork in the back look like a natural death,' she added dryly, enjoying his expression. 'It sounds to me that someone had listened to one too many of her angry tantrums. Gordon has let slip a few details about how volatile she is. I have a suspicion he's not just pulling his sister out of debt over here but setting up quite a stash for himself as well. I'm pretty sure he is quite smitten with me and its possible I feature in his future plans. He seems fairly disenchanted with married life back east.' She smirked slightly as she coolly shared the details.

'Let him keep thinking it,' Logan said coolly. 'As I said, I haven't got anything organised yet. There's no real rush if you can tolerate his attention for a while longer. In fact, I think we should take time to carefully set things up. You've found out a lot of background while you've been posing as his bit on the side in Perth. We're well-placed to set him up for a big fall. His wife's death might keep him busy for a while over there. Give us time to build a foolproof plan. I need to create a few links with the police, so I continue to look clean and upright. I want to keep a whole lot of distance between this and Logan Constructions. And I don't want any of the muck scraping off him onto us when he takes a fall. I want this to make an impact because I only want to do it once. Maximum effect, passing on a permanent message for anyone else who may think they can just casually walk in over here. This is our business,'

Logan continued forcefully. 'We put the effort into building it and I'll be damned if I'm going to sit back and let some blow-in from the east muscle in.'

'I quite agree,' Antonia nodded. 'I can handle him for a while longer. But the longer this goes on, the more it bites into our profits. I can't believe his was naïve enough to think he was coming up with an original idea! Once we get rid of him, we can move in on his sister, so it's our profit from her, not his.'

'And if we handle her properly, she'll be a lucrative source. I imagine he has already roped in some of her rich socialite friends. We can move them seamlessly over to us, a handy little future earner,' Logan mused. His cold eyes glistened at the thought. Throughout his career, Logan's infallible business plan was "never hold onto a losing scheme". His commercial success came through his determination to make each venture show maximum profit and drop it quickly if it didn't.

'Good idea.' Antonia was happy with the way their discussion had gone. They made an effective working partnership; both being committed exclusively to building their income and widening their positive profile in the affluent end of town. She closed the subject by urging, 'Drink up, I'm ready for another. And you can decide where we go for dinner.' Antonia watched Logan head to the bar, appreciating his attractive, suited figure. She found it hard work to maintain the façade of considerate companion with Gordon, he was so boring and full of himself. On the plus side, she enjoyed the luxury surroundings of the Crowne Plaza and his generosity. But maybe his generosity was just part of his method of winning her favour. *Oh well, all good things come to an end, Gordon,* she mused dispassionately.

On the long flight back to Sydney, Gordon had time to think about his current situation. He had gone to Perth all those months ago in answer to his sister's distress call. She had no money sense and had quickly wasted her inheritance maintaining her habitually extravagant lifestyle. Gordon had looked for an income stream that would keep Linda comfortable and require little maintenance once it was established. He had settled on a betting syndicate. He scouted through Linda's wealthy friends and called in old friends he'd made through the horse industry over the years. He charged everyone a sizeable compulsory membership fee, which he banked in a private bank account he opened for the purpose. He gambled a portion of the money, careful not to make too big a profit or loss. Thanks to all the online betting facilities, he could place his bets wherever he was in Australia. Membership required patrons to make ongoing deposits to maintain the balance of the account. On joining, they were promised an annual percentage of the profits. Some of the less-than-honest members indicated to Gordon that they would be happy to use the syndicate to launder their money rather than make a huge profit. Gordon understood what he was doing was barely legal but reasoned that with luck, it would suit until he had gathered reasonable nest eggs for himself and his sister that could be invested in more mainstream ventures. It suited him to pay low to some and higher to others as long as no one saw the books, because his private plan was to skim a regular amount from the account and put it in a separate account of his own. With Felicity owning Divine Hayfields, Gordon had reasoned his share in a divorce settlement would only be half the value of the stud and he'd have to fight hard even for that. He had decided the betting syndicate would give him a platform to start afresh if, or more likely when, he decided to leave her. With Felicity now out of the picture, he envisaged a substantial inheritance. He was quietly pleased with how well things were working out in Perth and meeting Antonia had been the cream on the cake so to speak. Little did he realise his first meeting with her was no accident and her demonstrated feelings of affection were as shallow as a clay pan on the Swan Coastal Plain.

Gordon frowned as his thoughts took a turn to the situation at Divine Hayfields. He was sure he had set everything up rock solid before he left. He couldn't think what had gone wrong for Felicity to be stabbed to death. *A pitchfork, no less!* He racked his brains to think who she could have enraged to that extent. He knew from years of navigating the most peaceful route through his marriage just how infuriating she could be. *Could she have upset Jarred? No, he had never shown any hint of being unable to work with her. Ali? Burt?* There seemed to be no reliable answer. This was most definitely not how Gordon had pictured his return home but, in some ways, Felicity's death in this manner would make it easier. On the other hand, he was not looking forward to all the police attention.

Gordon sighed as he accepted a drink from the airline steward. He suddenly couldn't face going all the way home tonight. He decided a night in the Meriton Suites at Mascot would help him regroup before heading to Divine

Hayfields tomorrow. He swallowed his drink and resolved to head to the hotel as soon as he picked up his luggage and retrieved his car from the long-term park.

CHAPTER TEN

Early next morning, Kaylee walked briskly into the station and was slightly put-out to see Ben there before her.

'Glad you could make it,' he teased. She snorted and spoke with mock grimness, 'Well since you've been here for hours apparently, what have you discovered?'

Ben had organised his notes from the previous day, using headings for Facts, Hearsay, Supposition, and No Idea.

Kaylee read over what he had written and was interested to note big question marks beside Darren, Kevin and Burt.

'We'll have to ask Mr Hathaway a few questions too, see if he can shed any light,' Kaylee mused. 'Why are you focused on Burt?'

'He just seemed overly stressed by our presence. More so than a man with nothing to hide. I'm also at a loss how to get Darren and Kevin to open up. They're both hiding something, that's for sure.'

Preliminary reports arrived then, complete with Clicks's and Paul's notes. The two detectives read through the notes and Ben shouted, 'Ha, I told you! Not killed by the pitchfork! I *knew* it looked wrong. Wow, this suggests she was poisoned! This is a new tilt!'

'So, killed twice. Poisoned and then stabbed. Why?'

'Two people involved?'

'Again, why? Says here she was, as we thought, already dead when she was struck with the pitchfork. What was the poison?'

'There are a few question marks there as well. We need some medical background on Mrs Hathaway.'

'Clicks and Paul didn't get anything off the pitchfork. In fact, there wasn't anything much out of the ordinary. So, we're no further along really. Looks like it's back to the farm for us. I can't see Mr Hathaway getting up here from Sydney too early so we'll have time to drop in on Mr Bunrack on our way,' Kaylee decided.

Kaylee called Clicks and Paul in. She gave them the search warrant and keys for Ali's house. She made some specific requests for things they should look out for, adding with a smile that as usual anything they could turn up was better than nothing. While she was busy with that, Ben strolled out to the front desk to see what had been discovered about Ali Hadji. He was not particularly surprised to learn that Ali had indeed left the country. It was not possible to find out if he had been travelling alone but it was confirmed he had flown to Damascus via Dubai. Ben made a mental note to follow that up with the police in Damascus. That would be a problem, there were no Arabic speakers in the station. They would probably have to find a translator in Newcastle or Sydney.

As Ben and Kaylee followed the scrub-lined road back out through Wheeler, Ben shared the latest news on Ali. They discussed his sudden flight but could not come up with any reasonable theories.

They turned in at the gates to Croham, bracing themselves for another encounter with fiery Gisella. She didn't disappoint them, appearing at the front door, with hands waving and a torrent of questions pouring off her tongue. Kaylee waited patiently for a break in the stream and asked firmly where they might find Burt. Into the flow of questions, Gisella inserted vague directions and gestured in the direction of the sheds. The two detectives thanked her and turned to skirt the house, their eyes fixed on their destination and their ears trying to block the diminishing confusion of questions, comments, and Italian exclamations.

'Goodness me!' Kaylee exclaimed, 'there sure are some mercurial women round her.' She caught sight of Burt working on a tractor and veered towards him.

'Hey, Burt,' she said.

Burt jumped and banged his head on the open hood of the tractor. 'What? What're ya think ya doin' creepin' up on a man?' he shouted, rubbing his head with a grease-covered hand.

'Sorry to startle you,' Ben said. 'We need a bit more information from you if you don't mind.'

'I've told you all I know!' he growled, still rubbing his head, and leaning against the tractor. Burt's heart sank, and he braced himself for more questions, knowing he would have to keep his wits when giving his answers.

'Burt, you seemed to be overly nervous when we were here yesterday, and I'd like to know why. You must understand, we are investigating the murder of your neighbour and of course we are a little worried when someone seems nervous,' Ben said, calculating that his words might jolt Burt into some form of cooperativeness. He was getting a bit tired of people who seemed to have so much to hide.

'Look, I've done nuthin',' Burt mumbled, while his brain worked feverishly to come up with something that would satisfy the police. 'She was a pain in the neck, and she made me damned mad, but I know better than to kill her. I'm not some hot-headed, thoughtless idiot. I know where killin' her would put me.'

'Okay, so you didn't kill Mrs Hathaway. But you have done something, haven't you Burt,' Ben risked a shot in the dark. Burt glanced up quickly, frowning. Ben decided that was a guilty face if ever he'd seen one and waited to see what Burt would say. The silence drew out.

'I wonder if Gisella could help us,' Ben turned to ask Kaylee to have a chat with her. It was too much for Burt.

'Wait, wait! No need to be bothering Gisella with anythin' now,' Burt blustered hastily. He flushed and paused, then opened his mouth with a calculating look on his face. Then he closed his mouth again.

'Well, what is it? We haven't got all day, so you better spill the beans,' Kaylee said sharply. She was amazed at the talent for evasiveness and downright lying shown by so many of the people they had interviewed in relation to this crime. *Maybe it's something to do with the country air,* she mused silently.

Burt sighed rather dramatically. 'Oh, Gisella. Good woman but she's got some pretty firm ideas about what we grow and sell,' Burt started slowly. 'A while ago, she wanted us to go into desserts, fancy stuff, grow berries and run dairy cows to make yoghurts and custards and cheeses. I reckon we've got our Captain Kirk cut out as it is ...'

'Wait a bit, Captain Kirk? What's that?'

'Eh? Oh, work. Anyway, who knows what she'd think up next if I gave in without a fight? Grapes? Wine? Those damned vegetables are pretty time-consuming as it is, ya know, and a real headache if we don't get rain when we need it. Or too much rain when we don't need it, for that matter. If we did her idea, we'd need to put on another man, set up a dairy, buy the herd. I ain't got time for dairyin' on top of everything else. It'd be good bugs bunny, sorry, money, when it was established but bloody costly to set up and a few lean years til it all came into top production. We were doin' ok, didn't need another string in the fiddle if ya know what I mean.' Once Burt began, the words came tumbling out more confidently. 'Anyway, couple years back things were tight because cattle prices dipped. We still sell the bulk of our beef through the sale yards, not direct to Sydney restaurants. I wanted a good cash crop that didn't need much work. Bloke in town asked if he could share-farm a potato crop up the back paddock. So, I said yeah if he did all the work and we split the profit 50-50.'

'So, does this fellow have a name?'

Burt paused for a beat. 'Ah, I only know his nickname. Ah, its Yanko.'

'That all? Just Yanko?' Kaylee prodded.

'Yeah. 'E button'oled me in town one day. I don't really know him.'

'So, you're happy to split the proceeds on the sale of the

spuds even though you don't know him? Stretching things a bit, aren't you?' Ben's frown creased his forehead.

'That's 'ow things work in the country,' Burt said quickly. He rushed on, 'Told him I didn't want Gisella knowing anythin' about it. She'd hit the roof if she knew I was growin' Spanish waiters when I'd put the kibosh on her fancy plans ...'

'Burt! Stop. Spanish waiters? Translate, please,' Kaylee's tone was impatient.

'What? Oh, sorry. Taters,' Burt said in a tone of voice that indicated any fool would know that. He continued, 'So, he's been goin' along fine, farmin' the waiters and I'm gettin' a nice little kickback. Don't really need it now cattle prices 'ave risen again but Gisella don't need to know about it. If she starts puttin' pressure on me about diversifyin' again, I might just say yes to one idea to keep her sweet. I can use the nest egg from the share-farming to tide us over.' Burt put on a sheepish voice as if embarrassed admitting that he tried to maintain marital peace. He thought he'd been clever to put in a bit of cockney rhyming slang to divert the cops.

'But Burt, why do you need to be obstructive with us over what is basically just a business decision? Share-farming wasn't illegal last time I looked,' Ben said.

'I got nothin' to hide, but with someone dead, there's no knowin' how far you lot will dig. Back home in Croydon, the damned space hoppers, sorry, coppers never stopped digging if they had a sniff of trouble. I didn't want your fellers swarming all over the place and Gisella finding out about the waiters. She can make life pretty bloody hard, ya know. That Felicity could be sheer hell but none of us here killed her, that's for sure. Not worth it. Anyway, Gisella's too soft hearted, Silvio wouldn't even know where to start, and I'm smart enough to stay out of trouble these days. Now, if ya don't mind, I'd better get crackin' on this tractor. Gotta harvest some of them vegetables tomorrow, they won't wait, and I don't want them spoiling.'

'Yes, Burt. I see what you mean about staying out of trouble. Just one more thing. You were ok about working with Gordon on this regeneration, were you? It's not an inconvenience you'd rather escape by killing Mrs Hathaway?'

'Hell no! Gordon's ok. We'll get the job done in no time now Felicity's not 'ere to raise objections. Like I said, not worth it to kill her,' Burt said shortly and turned back to the works under the hood of the tractor.

The detectives turned to go. Burt worked the spanner for a few seconds until he was sure the detectives were on their way. Then he turned and leant on the tractor to watch them, a rather crafty grin on his face. *That should keep them off my case,* he mused. Then he frowned. He really did not need any of this right now and was feeling nervous as well as frustrated. 'I'm getting' too old for this caper,' he muttered. *I might have to give my fat little sideline away and just keep the legit garden,* he thought regretfully.

'Our Burt must have had a colourful past back in merry England. Where now?' Ben said.

'Divine Hayfields, I guess,' Kaylee sighed. 'Why can't Burt grow potatoes in the market garden? Why does he need to keep them a secret? Do you really think he's growing potatoes?'

'Nah, not spuds. You can bet he's got a nice little sideline of marijuana on the go, hidden deep up the back paddock,' Ben chuckled casually.

'Ben! Really? Do you think Mrs Hathaway found out about it and was holding it over Burt so he killed her? We'll have to follow that up. Need to try and find this Yanko character.'

She changed the subject, 'Mr Hathaway might be home by now. If he isn't, Susannah might be able to help with her mother's medical history.'

'It was revealing, if not particularly helpful,' Ben chuckled. 'All these people hiding little things from each other! Crazy. Burt got over Mrs Hathaway's death pretty quickly, but I bet you anything he'll be at her funeral squeezing out a few crocodile tears.'

'It's a small community, Ben. They must keep up appearances. Among farming people, who knows when they'll be called on to lend a hand or when they'll be asking for a hand? It doesn't do any of them any good to be airing their grievances about each other. I'd also go as far as to say whoever rang the Police Help Line about the priest had some dispute with him, rather than anything concrete linking him to Mrs Hathaway's death. Mind you it doesn't help us much. We have all these suspects conveniently in the one area, except for Ali, and we can't make any headway. I know Ali leaving Australia in such a hurry looks pretty suspicious, but remember, he lives in the village, and he'd already gone home for the day.'

'He could easily have come back later. We've seen there's no security here. He could have left his car down the road and walked up.'

'What, walked up and poisoned Mrs Hathaway?'

'Yeah, when you put it like that, it sounds implausible. But what if he had already planned it with someone else? Kevin or Darren? You know, I thought when they called this thing in that it would be pretty quickly dealt with but even the autopsy threw up more questions than answers.' Ben sighed with frustration.

Pulling up at Divine Hayfields homestead, they stepped onto the veranda and knocked. The door was open as usual. *Another sign of non-existent security,* Kaylee thought. Shortly, Susannah appeared. She made the effort to appear welcoming and invited the detectives into the kitchen.

'Have you heard from your dad?' Kaylee opened the conversation.

'Yeah, he rang this morning. Said he couldn't face the drive up here last night. Should be here by about lunchtime, I'd say.'

'He's not exactly rushing back, is he?' Ben commented.

Susannah flushed, bristling at the criticism, even though it was what she had thought after speaking to her father. 'What could he achieve? He can't save Mum and Jarred has the farm under control.'

'Perhaps he could have made the effort to get here sooner to support you and Darren,' Kaylee murmured.

'Oh, well, what's done is done,' Susannah snapped impatiently. 'What can I help you with?'

'We'd like to look in your mother's bedroom if we could,' Ben said.

'What for? She was killed at the stables,' Susannah objected.

Ben briefly explained the forensic results that had already been gathered and asked whether Mrs Hathaway had been on any regular medication.

Susannah frowned. She said her mother was usually in good health, only suffering from occasional insomnia. She took prescription sedatives for that on an "as needed" basis.

'Anything else?' Ben pressed.

'Oh yes,' Susannah's brow cleared. 'I forgot. She went over to England last month, looking at horses, of course. She developed a blood clot on the return flight. They put her in hospital in Sydney. You can imagine how she raged about that! So, they said if she could give herself the anticoagulant injections, they'd let her come home so long as she stayed in regular touch with her GP. Naturally, she quickly proved to them in the hospital that she was perfectly capable of injecting herself, so they let her come home. As far as I know she had been giving herself the needles every evening.'

'Was she staying in touch with her doctor? What's his name?'

'I think so. Doctor Graham, in the medical centre in Muswellbrook. I think she saw him last week,' Susannah's forehead wrinkled a little as she thought.

'We need to look at her medications to get the names and give them to the forensic people.'

Susannah sighed and led the way to her mother's bedroom, pointing out the ensuite and her mother's side of the bed where her personal essentials could be found. The bedside drawer held an eye mask, moisturiser in a tube, notebook and pen, a well-thumbed novel and a box containing ten or a dozen commercially prepared Heparin injections. Ben pulled on gloves and took a snap lock bag out of his pocket. He raised his eyebrows at Kaylee, and she nodded. He collected the medication from the bedside table. Moving on to the bathroom drawers, he found, every woman's necessities including hair gel, headache tablets, make-up and deodorant, plus Ambien tablets in a flat box. He gathered up the Ambien and the headache tablets, sealing the bag carefully.

As they left the bedroom, a vehicle could be heard pulling up outside.

CHAPTER ELEVEN

'That's Dad,' Susannah said, hurrying towards the veranda. Ben and Kaylee hung back to allow Susannah and her father to greet each other. She hugged her father and clung to him for a while before stepping away. They spoke briefly, then Susannah indicated the detectives on the veranda and said to her father, 'They need to ask you some questions.'

Gordon Hathaway held out his hand to shake. 'Come in and sit down,' he said briskly. 'Let's not string this out. I'm happy to help in any way I can to find my wife's killer, but I have a stud farm to run.'

Huh, thought Ben sardonically, *you've got a stud farm to run now, but when you wanted to travel to Perth it was ok to leave it in the hands of the wife and the manager.*

Kaylee frowned as she sat down on a veranda chair, thinking that Mr Hathaway was either hiding his grief well or was not particularly saddened by his wife's death. Susannah quietly left them to it and walked to her room, pulling out her phone as she did so.

When can I see you? she texted.

Immediately her phone pinged a reply. *Now, at Thompson's.* She ran a brush through her hair and grabbed her purse and keys.

As she stepped past her father and the detectives on the veranda, she said briefly, 'I'm just going to pick up a couple of things from the store. Do you want anything, Dad?'

'No. You know what's needed. I'll see you at dinner tonight. I'll scratch something together for lunch if you're not back by then.' He waved briefly and turned back to the detectives.

They found not much new in his answers to their questions. He had been in Perth for a week. He said there could be any number of people his wife had upset. In his nightly calls to Felicity, he hadn't heard of any fresh quarrels while he was away. Their call on the night of her death had been brief and mundane. He confirmed Susannah's account of Felicity's blood clot on her return from England. He said her last visit to the doctor had been positive, adding that he thought Felicity would have been on the heparin for about another month. When questioned about his relationship with his wife, he frowned and spoke heavily. 'Felicity and I were married twenty-six years ago. Anyone can tell you we rowed all the time, but we were still together, we made a good team. We had some great times, we were successful. We never let the day end on a fight. I must admit, I had learnt some peace-keeping techniques,' he smiled sardonically, 'and I also learnt to compromise, something Felicity wasn't much good at.'

'We've taken your wife's medication and I'll get you to sign for it,' Kaylee said. She sensed Gordon stiffen but when she glanced at him, his face was impassive.

She offered the docket, and he signed his name, standing

as he pocketed the pen. 'If that's all, I really need to get down to the stables and catch up with my manager. This must have been difficult for him,' he said briskly. He strode purposefully towards the stables, every inch the confident, wealthy landowner.

In her car, Susannah turned the air conditioner full on even though the day was not hot. She felt rattled and on edge. She thought the cool breeze on her face might have a settling effect. She couldn't wait to see Silvio and escape from all the awful thoughts that were swirling through her mind. She realised she would not be able to stay long with him because everyone knew that a run to Wheeler store and back only took thirty to forty minutes. She glanced ahead and in the rear-view mirror to check no one would see her turn into Thompson's farm. Her heart skipped a beat when she realised Mr Thompson could possibly be working at the property. She drove carefully round the back, quickly inventing a reason to be visiting. She was relieved to see Silvio's bike and no sign of Mr Thompson.

Silvio held her in a tight hug, then they walked onto Mr Thompson's veranda, sitting together on the old two-seater swing chair.

'I can't stand this,' she sighed. 'I hate all the sneaking 'round. Everything is up in the air, I miss mum. Dar's no support, just hides in his room. I wish we could get away, just the two of us, go to the coast, swim, let the surf wash everything away. Could we get away?'

Silvio slid his arm round her shoulder, and she leant into him. His mind was racing. He would love to have Zanna all to himself, with no sneaking around and no responsibilities.

It would be a wonderful opportunity to see how they got on together in a neutral situation. He pictured them waking up together and taking long walks to breakfast cafes before spending the morning on the beach. He imagined them dining on the waterfront in the evenings. The thoughts were exciting and a little bit scary when he realised just how far their relationship had progressed. *Could this be it? Am I in love with her?*

He said cautiously, 'We could go for a few days if we left on Sunday morning. I have to help hand out fliers promoting Croham Foods at the fundraiser on Saturday night.'

Susannah jumped. 'I'd forgotten about that damned thing. Mum was serving steak sandwiches at the produce store barbeque. I suppose I will either have to make our apologies for that or take her place.'

'No big deal, sweetheart. Let's get the fundraiser out of the way and just take off early Sunday morning. No need to tell anyone where we're going. They'll only raise a stink. What about your mum's funeral?'

'We can't organise anything until the police release her and they reckon they still have things to investigate,' she said sadly. Then she rallied. 'Ok, the fundraiser is tomorrow night. We're off after that. I'm packing a bikini and a beach towel and that's all! I'm supposed to be on my way to Wheeler now, so I'll fuel up the car and we can be away quickly on Sunday morning. Where shall we go? Forster, Port Macquarie, Ballina? This is exciting.' She snuggled up closer and he squeezed her to his side.

'I'll walk out to the road and start towards Wheeler at

half-six. Then you can pick me up when you come along. What about Port Macquarie? Which way will we go? Tamworth and then down the Oxley highway?' Silvio said enthusiastically. 'There's a great range of accommodation at Port, and there'll be plenty of tourists, even this early in the season. We can just merge in.' Silvio rattled on rapidly as his excitement grew.

'Yes! I love that road, all the twists and turns, and you feel as if you're not getting anywhere and then suddenly there you are at the coast. That's a road that will certainly clear my head.' Susannah sat up, remembering the road she had travelled often with her family when they went to the coast for holidays.

'Why will it clear your head?'

'The mountain climbs, the curves. I call roads like that "good for the soul" because in some spots you're almost praying you'll make it! It takes a lot of concentration to drive it.'

Silvio grinned slyly. 'I'd better not distract you, then.'

'Oh,' Susannah blushed and laughed, 'I do love you!' She spoke impulsively, throwing herself back into his arms.

Surprised at himself, Silvio found himself saying, 'I love you, too.' They shared a long kiss.

After a few moments, Susannah broke away and said, 'I'd better get along. We can text if anything comes up. Otherwise, I'll see you tomorrow night at the fundraiser.'

'Take it easy, sweetheart. I'll text you tonight.' Silvio gave her a last kiss and saw her into her car. Susannah glanced back down the road before driving out and waited for the approaching car to pass. She recognised the detectives' car and breathed silent thanks that her car was mostly screened by the trees, and she hadn't left a few moments earlier. She let the dust settle for a bit, waved to Silvio and drove towards Wheeler.

Silvio stared after her with a bemused expression on his face. He'd said he loved her, it just slipped out. *Do I really love her?* He tried to analyse his feelings. He knew there was a strong physical attraction between them. He knew he felt very protective of her, wanting to shield her from the horror of her mother's death and all the terrible fallout from that. *Is that love? What if I'm just enjoying being with Susannah because if is frowned on by my parents and hers?* He thought his feelings were stronger than that. *Do I want to spend the rest of my life with her?* That was an extremely attractive prospect. *Maybe I really am in love.* He had a nagging feeling that it was wrong to leave without letting their families know, but he wanted to be with Zanna away from all the drama and upheaval that was going on at her place and his. Something was bugging his dad, he knew. *Was Dad involved in Mrs Hathaway's death? What a terrible thought!* Mama, also, was behaving rather oddly but he couldn't work out if that was because she, too, knew something was eating away at Burt, or because she was still digesting his own revelation about Susannah. Maybe going away would give his parents a chance to regroup and sort out what was bothering them. He sighed, then kicked the motorbike to life and rode thoughtfully home.

Gordon searched briefly through the stables before finding Jarred in the exercise yard, working with a handsome, leggy chestnut. Gordon ran an assessing eye over the yearling, impressed with the action and the confidence in its paces. He reflected with satisfaction that Jarred was indeed completely capable of keeping things going in his absence.

Jarred saw him and shortened the lunging rope, gradually pulling the horse to him and slowing it to a walk. He greeted Gordon with relief, indicating that the session with the animal was over and heading to the stable. He called out to Taj as they entered the stables and handed him the rope so he could attend to grooming and cool the sweating creature down.

'Come up to the house,' Gordon said. 'We can talk there. You can fill me in on things.'

They sat on the veranda, looking out across the property. Jarred listened to the magpies for a moment while he gathered his thoughts then began to speak. He gave a concise account of the last two days. Then, with obvious reluctance, he mentioned that Hamish had quit, and Ali had disappeared. In the interest of keeping nothing from his boss, he added the news of Ali's axe-throwing course. He wondered briefly what the police were making of that nugget of information. Gordon swore, frowning at the implications of one of his staff knowing how to throw an axe and of being short-handed to the tune of not one but two staff members. Belatedly he realised that Felicity had been very hands on as well.

'Who do you think did this to Felicity?' he asked Jarred bluntly. 'Do you think it was Ali? What about Hamish? Was there trouble while I was away?'

'I don't know what to think about Ali. There didn't seem

to be anything going on. Felicity was riding them all hard, as she does … did. But they all seemed to be handling it. They only get rebellious when they are not kept busy and have time to brood. Believe me, we all had plenty of work to keep us occupied. And it will be much worse now we're two men down. I can come up with no reason for Ali to just clear off like that. Maybe the axe-throwing thing has nothing to do with anything. I thought he seemed happy enough, but I didn't know him all that well. He was pretty quiet,' Jarred said thoughtfully.

'Well, what about Hamish?' Gordon barked impatiently.

'Oh, he's just a weak kid. He was scared, and the others are not inclined to be sympathetic. I had to decide whether to keep him and be prepared to spend time propping him up or let him go. I really didn't think I had time to be shielding him from the others' harassment with everything else going on. The harassment wasn't deliberately malicious, just the usual hard-hearted treatment that happens to every weak worker everywhere. I told him I'd give him a good reference and let him go. He lacked initiative and I had hoped he would develop some while working here, but the way things have worked out, I haven't got time now. I've lined up Jason to come every day until further notice, probably after the sales,' Jarred paused, thinking. 'I dunno, really, probably just best to keep going as per the program and let the police do their thing. Have you got anyone in mind that we could put on to help with the workload, or should we get Darren to advertise the position? Hiring could be a problem as news of Felicity's death spreads. We'll have to weed out the ones who apply for curiosity, and some good hands might be put off applying.'

'Damn it all!' Gordon burst out. Fresh implications resulting from Felicity's murder kept occurring to him. What a messy business it was becoming. 'Okay, let me sound out a few of the owners round about and see if they can suggest anyone. I guess you're right about just carrying on. I just hate all the uncertainty and I'll have to go back to Perth in a few weeks. Oh well, you'd best get on. I'll go over and see Burt,' he said more reasonably and stood up.

Jarred stepped off the veranda, his mind already occupied with re-allocating and prioritising tasks.

CHAPTER TWELVE

Kaylee turned to Ben as he drove them back to the station. 'What do you make of the Ali Hadji axe-throwing thing? Is it anything or nothing? Is axe-throwing the same as pitchfork-throwing?'

'I don't think it's much. A pitchfork is pretty much the same weight all the way along. An axe is heavy at one end and would be thrown so it goes end-over-end. A pitchfork would be thrown more like a javelin. They are two separate styles of throwing. Anyway, I reckon the pitchfork was thrust into her when she was down rather than thrown into her.'

'I bow to your judgement. But we will keep it in mind. Were you serious about going to the fundraiser? It's tomorrow night.'

'I know. Yeah, I think we could maybe find out something by attending,' he replied.

'Will you have a date, Ben?' She glanced sideways at him, with a half-smile on her face.

'Nah. We'll be sort of working, wouldn't be fair to any of my many female admirers,' Ben smirked. 'I'll give you a ride if you're going solo.'

'That'll be great. Pick me up about half-seven. I'm going to try to fit in like a local and buy jam and pickles and produce and put them in my string bag.' Kaylee giggled quietly. 'I think I'll try my luck with some of their food stalls, too.' She felt a little excited at the prospect of wandering through a night market. She knew she would stay alert with her police officer self still switched on and observant, but she was also determined to enjoy the evening.

On Saturday night, they drove into Wheeler and discovered they had to search for parking, every available spot being taken up by early birds. Inside and outside the church hall a crowd of people milled among the market stalls, browsing and chatting, stopping to greet friends. Fairy lights were strung about outside, their feeble light supported by strategically placed floodlights. Aromatic smoke drifted up from several food stalls. Music played, not quite in the background, but not loud enough to make conversation difficult. Flocks of children ran about in the open areas, squealing and playing chasey, happy to be on the loose with their friends in the balmy evening air.

Kaylee quickly recognised the vicar, Mac Brennan with a woman (his wife?), Kevin Craig, all three Hathaways, and the owner of the general store. There were many other friendly and relaxed faces, people ready to enjoy an evening of fun catching up with friends and escaping from the cares of rural life and the boring routine of planning and cooking the evening meal. The atmosphere was cheerful and casual. Most of the women seemed ready to settle in for a good gossip, maybe a little discreet speculation about Mrs Hathaway's death because the news had floated round the village as news does in country towns. They relaxed, content that their children were safe, and their men were occupied, and everyone could be fed easily. Small groups were gathered on picnic rugs or were sitting on camp chairs with friends, balancing plates on their knees. Others strolled along the row of market stalls, inspecting the wares and making purchases.

As she and Ben wandered through, Kaylee stopped for a quick word of greeting with Susannah Hathaway. She thought Susannah seemed a little tense, but mentally shrugged it off, reasoning that it was a difficult time for Susannah just now. Ben continued strolling, his eyes fixed on Kevin Craig. He hoped that Kevin might be inclined to be more talkative in this relaxed atmosphere and he still had some questions he wanted to ask the specialist groom. Kevin casually walked round the corner of the hall, into a darker area, away from the main throng of people. Ben followed and was in time to see Kevin's face glow in a match flash as he lit a cigarette.

'Hey, Kevin,' he said in a casual, friendly voice.

'Oh, hi, er, Ben,' Kevin replied, exhaling smoke. He seemed unsure whether to be friendly or more formal with the policeman in this setting.

'Pretty good turnout for the fundraiser,' Ben commented as an opener.

Kevin nodded, 'Not bad.'

'I know you're not in working hours,' Ben began. 'But I wondered if you'd care to walk and talk.'

Kevin nodded noncommittally. They took a few steps deeper into the shadows.

'I wonder ...' Ben started.

He got no further with his question. Something crashed

hard into the side of his head. He crumpled forward onto the grass next to the ceramic pot plant that had been used to bash him unconscious.

Kevin leapt over Ben's body, grabbing the arm of the assailant, hissing savagely, 'What the hell are you doing? You damned fool!'

He dragged the slighter man roughly away into the deep shadows behind the church under the oak tree.

'What were you thinking? You've just clobbered a cop, for God's sake!'

Darren turned and fell into Kevin's arms, gasping unevenly. 'I saw you talking. I didn't want him asking you any more questions,' he said weakly.

Kevin could feel Darren shaking. He hugged him, stroking his back. He knew he needed to soothe Darren before he could talk sense into him.

'Shh, lover, just breathe for a bit. Calm down. Did you come in your own car?' he asked softly, trying to keep his voice low and calm.

'No. Zanna and Dad and I all came up together. We were going to have a fairly short evening, but Dad still wanted us to "be a presence" as he put it.'

'Well you can't run off home without your own wheels. You'll have to pull yourself together and try to act normal,' Kevin said trying to sound reassuring.

'Oh God,' Darren gulped. 'How?' He sank against Kevin's chest, wrapping his thin arms around the taller man.

Kevin's reply was cut off by a piercing scream rising above the music. 'Help! Help! Someone's been hurt! Help!'

Kaylee heard the scream and ran towards it. She rounded the corner of the hall where two or three others had gathered around Ben, still unconscious on the ground.

Her heart lurched when she recognised Ben. 'I'm a police officer. Stand back, will you,' she commanded loudly as she knelt beside him, feeling his neck for a pulse. With relief, she felt the steady beat. She sensed someone kneeling beside her and was thankful to hear a strong calm voice saying, 'I'm with the ambulance. Luckily, we're attending this event as a safety requirement. Let's see what's happened. Can you focus your torch on the victim, please?'

Kaylee held her phone, so the built-in torch lit Ben's upper body. The ambulance officer had been joined by a second officer. She left them to make their examination, sitting back on her heels and looking around. She noted the pot on the ground. She made a guess it had been used on Ben's head. She could think of no other reason why a fit young man like Ben would lose consciousness. Nor could she explain why a plant pot would be lying abandoned on the ground.

Someone came round the side of the building with a portable floodlight, relieving Kaylee of torch-holding duties. She edged round and discretely pushed the pot into her string bag, trying not to touch it. *I'll get this checked for fingerprints,* she thought grimly.

Behind the church, Darren clung to Kevin, breathing shakily. 'Come with me,' Kevin whispered urgently, pulling Darren after him. He hoped everyone would be focused on Ben and they could get to his car unnoticed. He knew he didn't have much time to calm Darren sufficiently so he could return unobtrusively to the crowd.

'Come on, get in, little Dar. Try to relax. Bloody hell! What a damn fool thing to do,' he muttered.

Darren slumped in the passenger seat. 'I'm sorry,' he moaned. 'I'm sick of trying to remember what to say and what not to say. I'm sick of lying. I just wish this mess would go away,' he sighed.

'Look, it'll be ok. You know you didn't kill your mother. Just keep focused on that. Stay under the radar, act normal. Not like tonight! God!' Kevin slapped his forehead in frustration. He went on quickly in a quiet voice, 'Don't do anything like that again. It was so stupid. We must get back to the crowd. If your dad asks why you're upset, just tell him your mother's death keeps catching up with you. Go now, my little hunky Dar. I'll see you at home later.' He gave Darren a reassuring squeeze and kissed him gently.

Darren clutched at Kevin's arm, but Kevin pushed him out of the car, whispering 'You'll be ok, lover. Be calm.'

Darren glanced doubtfully and Kevin waved reassuringly.

He waited until he saw Darren reach the market stalls. He felt pleased with his handling of Darren, although he was troubled that Darren had felt such drastic action was necessary. It felt good to take charge and comfort Darren, although Kevin had some very uneasy feelings about his actions and the whole situation. He thought briefly about his childhood and how he'd always tried to stay out of trouble to avoid nasty repercussions with his father. *Well, I'm deep in trouble now, and getting deeper,* he thought ruefully. He squared his shoulders and walked casually back to where he had been talking to Ben. His mind was spinning, trying to come up with a reasonable excuse for leaving Ben unconscious. He could see that Ben had recovered and was sitting with his back against the hall. Most of the crowd had lost interest and wandered back to the marketplace, leaving Kaylee, the vicar and the two ambulance men with Ben.

Kevin walked over and squatted beside Ben. He tried for a friendly tone, 'You all right, mate?' he asked solicitously. 'I chased the bastard (sorry, Vicar), but he was too quick for me.'

Ben nodded, then winced. 'Did you get a look at him?'

'Nah, 'fraid not. Pretty dark out here and he scarpered off behind the church.'

Even through the throbbing in his head, Ben registered surprise that Kevin was too slow to catch his attacker. He was not convinced by Kevin's admission. 'Ah well, leave it. Thanks for trying. You get back to your evening out. I might call it a night,' he said.

Kaylee privately agreed this was the best course to take. She turned to the ambulance men, 'Will he be right to go now?'

'Yes. He'll have a sore head for a bit. I'd say take it easy for twenty-four hours, avoid alcohol. If you have persistent headache or disorientation, see your doctor or go to Emergency in Muswellbrook hospital.'

'Ok, thanks,' Ben said. He tried to stand, and a sharp arrow of pain shot through his head. 'Give us a hand up, could you?' He tried to keep his voice light and held his hand out to Kaylee.

They thanked the ambulance officers and slowly made their way down the road to where Ben had left his car.

'You ok?' Kaylee queried, holding out her hand for his car keys.

'Yeah, a quiet evening and a good night's sleep and I'll be right as rain,' Ben's voice was confident but he wondered if that was true, feeling his head pounding in time with his heart.

'I didn't get to do any shopping or even eat,' Kaylee complained. 'Why did you have to get yourself whacked?'

'Like I would choose to get a bang on the head like that! Bloody hell, it hurt.'

'Yeah, well, time to get serious. I'll drive you back to your place and we'll pick up a pizza on the way. Then we can have an exchange of ideas about this evening because I can tell you have one or two question marks in your mind, and I *certainly* do. I also have a plant pot to take in for fingerprinting tomorrow,' Kaylee said with satisfaction.

'Is that what it was?' Ben asked vaguely.

Back at Ben's place, he swallowed a couple of painkillers, opened a beer for Kaylee and they settled down on his lounge with the pizza.

'Did you find out anything at all from Kevin?' Kaylee asked.

'No. I just got as far as suggesting we walk and talk and then *bang*! I think Kevin had just moved away from the crowd for a smoke ... unless he had arranged to meet someone round the back.'

'That sounds quite likely. The person he was meeting was the one who bashed you, I'd say. But who? Why? It's a fairly risky move to be knocking a cop on the head.'

'Seems quite a random and unplanned attack. I'm fairly

sure that whoever it was didn't outrun Kevin. I mean, look at him, young, fit, accustomed to running after horses. He must have a fair turn of speed. I'd say he caught my mugger and cleverly got him out of harm's way before coming back to me. I'm no further along at all, dammit. Who was he meeting? Why hit me?'

They tossed ideas back and forth for a while, but Kaylee could see that even though he was trying to seem on top of it, Ben's head wound was making its presence felt. She cleaned up after their meal, checked that Ben was going to bed, then called a cab to go home.

CHAPTER THIRTEEN

Ben's head still throbbed next morning, and he felt a tender spot when he ran the comb through his hair after his shower. His thoughts about muggers were far from generous, and he was relieved it was Sunday and not necessary to stick to formal work hours.

While Ben slowly pulled his mind into some semblance of working order, Silvio and Susannah were well on their way to Port Macquarie. Susannah was cheerfully driving, showing her usual flair for speed, but somewhat restricted by the heavy traffic on the mountainous highway to Tamworth. She was amazed at how the change of scenery had lightened her mood. Beside her, Silvio lounged back grinning and taking in the scenery. She thought back to her last holiday and was slightly stunned to think it was more than eighteen months ago. She'd taken a four-day weekend in Sydney with classmates after completing her studies at Charles Sturt University and since then had been immersed in life on Divine Hayfields. She was amazed how much time she had allowed to pass without job hunting in Queensland as had been her intention after graduating. A wry smile crossed her face as it dawned on her that despite the friction in the house, she had been happy working at home. She glanced at Silvio and realised their developing relationship was a major factor contributing to her happiness. *Is our romance "true love", or the result of two healthy young people with few other people our age for social contact?* she wondered. She knew she felt very strongly about Silvio, and she was fairly sure he felt the same way. Her mind wandered, happily daydreaming a future with Silvio until his shout brought her back to earth.

'Look out, Zanna! Slow down!' A car towing a caravan was slowly crawling in front of them up the hill. Heart pounding, Susannah braked hard and followed more cautiously until they could find a place to overtake. She glanced at Silvio, sitting bolt upright, eyes wide.

'Sorry, mind was wandering,' she murmured.

'Are you tired? Do you want me to drive?' Silvio turned in his seat, massaging her shoulder gently.

'No,' Susannah replied. 'Let's just wait for a passing lane to get ahead of this slowcoach and I promise I'll keep my mind on the job.' She gave him a weak grin. 'I was sort of daydreaming about the future,' she added.

He turned seriously to her. 'Do I feature in that future?' he asked shyly.

Impulsively, Susannah reached over and squeezed his arm. 'Actually, you do,' she said smiling.

'Well, let's concentrate on getting to the coast in one piece and then we can try a small taste of our future,' Silvio grinned, with a sense of happy anticipation.

* * *

In his kitchen, Ben certainly wasn't feeling any sense of happy anticipation as his phone rang sending a jabbing pain through his head.

'How's the head?' Kaylee enquired chirpily.

'All right, if you stop shouting,' Ben groaned.

She laughed. 'Stop being such a sook! Shall I come over and cook breakfast for the invalid and then we can compare notes?'

'Sure, so long as it's not invalid food like chicken broth and coddled eggs!'

A short time later, Kaylee was in the kitchen frying up bacon, eggs, tomato and sausage, demanding Ben take on the job of barista.

As they ate, they continued to speculate on the murder and their list of suspects.

'Didn't exactly turn out to be the big fact-finding mission we thought it would be last night, did it?' Ben said round a mouthful of sausage.

'What did you *really* say to Kevin?'

'Nothing at all! I just suggested a walk and talk, trying to keep it informal, and then, WHAM! Odd though don't you think that Kevin couldn't run down whoever it was who hit me? He's very fit ...'

'Agreed,' Kaylee said promptly. 'So, it was obviously someone Kevin knew and he's covering for them.'

'Who would he want to protect?'

'We may know more after I get that plant pot dusted for prints,' Kaylee suggested. 'There are so many loyalties, so many lies, so many people hiding things from each other and from us. Nothing is straightforward!' She banged her fork on the table in frustration.

Ben summarised: 'There are at least two people who feel strongly enough to kill Felicity. The one who threw the pitchfork into her and the one who poisoned her. How was that achieved? Her supper? Her wine? Her medication? We have Burt hiding something, possibly illegal, from Gisella. Silvio may or may not be keeping some facts to himself. Susannah was not giving us the full story about her father's Perth trips, but maybe she didn't know and was putout that it reflected rather badly on her father that he didn't share with her. Is Gordon simply going to Perth to help his sister? Or is there something else going on over there? I noticed him tense a bit when we mentioned poison but that's not conclusive. Darren is holding some cards close to his chest, as is Kevin. I think the vicar is straight, can't really see a man of God killing someone just because she got under his skin. Jarred told me that young Hamish has quit. Is that because he knows something? Or has done something? Or ... what? I frankly think he's not a candidate for strong consideration but at least we should be able to find him if we need to. We can't even *find out* if Ali has any secrets because his disappearance overseas is one big secret. We could just go round and round all day and still get nowhere.' He sighed, irritated that they were making no progress and his head was still aching.

'Did you do anything about contacting the police in Damascus? You might be lucky to find someone who speaks English, rather than tracking down an interpreter.'

'Wherever he is over there, he's probably safe and sound and cosily asleep right now. They're seven hours behind us, so assuming office hours start at nine, I'll try to call them round three or four tomorrow afternoon,' Ben said. He didn't have much hope of finding one man in a city of over three million inhabitants, and who was to say that Ali had stayed in Damascus at all? Maybe he had headed out into the countryside after his plane landed. *Too many possibilities,* Ben thought, discouraged.

Contrary to Ben's assumption, Ali was not sleeping safe and cosy. He was lying wide awake, his bed a mess from his tossing and turning. His mind swirled with unanswered questions, uncertainty and awful anxiety. He had caught a taxi from the airport to his family home after the plane landed and he cleared customs. His father and brothers had been very happy to see him and gave him welcoming hugs. But their conversation had quickly turned to their troubles. Although they were glad to have Ali with them, they were unable to find solace or solid answers. He groaned and rolled out of bed, heading to the coffee machine in the kitchen, sure that he would not catch another wink of sleep. His brothers and father were sitting at the table, looking haggard and unshaven, their hands wrapped around tiny steaming cups. They glanced up at Ali. His father waved vaguely towards the coffee machine while a brother pushed a chair out with his toe for Ali to sit.

'I can't stand this!' Ali burst out. He had assumed that being in his homeland and close to his family would bring him some comfort and was distressed to find how wrong he'd been.

His father frowned heavily, 'None of us can, son. It's a terrible situation but at least we have you here safe with us. We will just have to take it one day at a time and try to find a way through. You did right coming straight home to us. Lucky really, to have got on a plane so quickly. Together we can look after each other while we wait and figure out what's best to do.'

He had barely finished speaking when the phone rang. He snatched it up. 'Hello? Yes ... yes. Thank you.'

He disconnected the call and visibly pulled himself together, standing straighter and squaring his shoulders. He picked up the car keys.

'Come, sons. Now we must go.'

Ali seemed to shrink in despair. His tired eyes searched his father's face but found no comfort. The father held his arms wide and briefly embraced his sons. Unspeaking, they headed out to the car.

* * *

Far removed from cares and anxiety, Silvio and Susannah drove into Tamworth, looking for a spot to stop for a break.

As they sipped steaming coffees and watched the passing pedestrians, Susannah checked her phone for messages.

'Huh, no one has even missed me yet,' she complained.

'That's got to be a good thing, sweetheart. The longer we are not missed, the better.'

Susannah's excited mind skipped to another idea: 'Did you book anywhere for us to stay?'

'Nah, I think we should be able to find somewhere when we get there. There's plenty available and quite a variety of types of accommodation.'

'Ok, I'll leave that to you. Just so long as we don't wind up in a tent!' Susannah grinned.

Silvio stared at his phone in front of him, then spoke slowly. 'Will you answer if they start to panic and try to call you?' His brow wrinkled as he applied the question to his own situation.

Susannah replied soberly, 'Let's just stay out of touch with *everyone* at least until tomorrow. After we've had a peaceful night and a leisurely breakfast, maybe we'll have the stomach to field their questions. I'm just going to have my mind fixed on you and me and relaxing away from all the hassles.'

'I agree. Mum will be screaming loud enough not to need a phone!'

'Let's switch off our phones together and turn them on together tomorrow.' They bent their heads to their phones.

'Drink up and let's get going, we've had the regulation break. Three and a half hours to the beach!!' They hurried back to the car, both feeling renewed excitement in their plans.

* * *

At Croham, Gisella roamed restlessly around the house, continually stopping at Silvio's closed bedroom door. In the sunroom, she fidgeted with tiny ornaments, straightening them needlessly. Her worried frown deepened as Burt stepped noisily in from the garden. 'Have you seen Silvio this morning?' she demanded without greeting her husband.

'No,' he replied shortly. 'Did 'e say he was going anywhere after that do last night?'

'He say nothing to me,' she said. 'I thought he come straight home,' she paused before going on, 'What strange thing, someone to hit the policeman on the head. Who do something like that? Getting bad here. First Felicity murdered and now someone hits the policeman!' She shuddered. 'I don't like it, don't feel safe. We need to start locking up in the night.'

'Pretty silly thing to do, bashing a cop. Small town, people talk. Whoever did it will get caught for sure.'

Suddenly Gisella gasped. 'Maybe Silvio bashed policeman and now he run away!'

'Don't be stupid, woman! Why would he bash the cop? 'Ave you even checked if he's 'ere or not? Maybe 'e's just sleeping in. Go and look in his room.'

Gisella rushed away. Moments later, Burt heard her scream and wasted no time following her to Silvio's room.

'Oh, my baby, my boy! Caro, what stupid thing you do? He not here!' Gisella wailed.

Burt put his arms round her, taking in the unmade, empty bed. 'Stop fussin' woman. Why would our boy do anything stupid like runnin' away? Come on, love, stop the noise.' Burt thought quickly, then said, 'We can phone 'im, simple!'

He sagged with relief as he felt some of his wife's tension ease. She stopped moaning and fixed on that idea. She broke from his arms and rushed back to the sunroom to grab her phone.

With rapid fingers, Gisella selected her son's number

from her list of favourites, and waited, steadily growing more frantic as Silvio failed to answer. As his phone went to message bank, she gave vent to another wail and threw the phone down. Burt was at his wit's end. He always lost the power of sensible thought in the face of Gisella's histrionics.

'Wait, love! Wait. Stop crying. For God's sake, please stop crying! I can't think with your noise.'

He pushed his wife down into a lounge chair, and, completely disregarding the early hour of the day, quickly poured a sherry from the decanter. 'Drink this up. It'll settle you down and then I can think. Ah hell, what a mess! Where can that dratted boy be?'

Gisella gasped as the alcohol hit the back of her throat. She wiped her cheeks and looked with big sad eyes at Burt, silently begging him to find a solution to her son's absence.

After a few seconds, he suggested, 'He said 'e's seeing Susannah. Maybe 'e's stayed with 'er last night.'

'Oh Dio! No! Sleeping in sin? No, not my son!' The hysteria quickly resurfaced. Burt panicked.

'STOP!' he yelled. 'Stop and let me think, will you?' Gisella was shocked into silence. Burt spoke rapidly, trying to be gentle despite feeling so anxious, 'Now isn't the time to be thinking about that sort of thing. We've got bigger problems to deal with. I'll ring Gordon. You finish that drink and concentrate on calming yourself down.'

He slowly went to the telephone, numbed by this turn of events.

'Gordon Hathaway speaking,' his clear voice easily came through the phone to Burt.

Suddenly Burt felt somewhat unsure of himself, 'Ah,

Gordon. Burt 'ere. Ah, I was wonderin' if, ah, you've seen Susannah this mornin' at all?'

'No, can't say I have. I imagine she's still sleeping.'

'Could you, ah, check? If you don't mind, that is.'

'Why would I need to check? What's your problem, Burt?' Gordon asked sharply.

'Well, ah, the thing is, ah, she and Silvio 'ave been seein' each other and ...' Burt trailed off, unsure how to continue.

'What? What nonsense! Susannah wouldn't be seeing Silvio. Where'd you get that stupid idea?' Gordon didn't bother to hide his disbelief. *Burt must be dreaming,* he thought.

'Silvio said!' Burt raised his voice, nettled by Gordon's instant dismissal of the idea. His indignation allowed him to rush on, 'We 'aven't seen 'im this morning and we thought he might be at your place with Susannah.'

'Well, just to put an end to this stupid line of thought I *will* go and check her room,' Gordon said forcefully. 'Hang on, will you,' he added brusquely. Burt heard Gordon's footsteps echo distantly on the tiles and then return more hurriedly.

'She's not here, and her car's not out the front. You'd better come up here and we can discuss this.' He disconnected the call without waiting for Burt to reply.

CHAPTER FOURTEEN

urt and Gisella quickly drove the short distance to Divine Hayfields, pulling up at the front of the homestead. Gordon stood at the top of the steps frowning forbiddingly. Gisella took a few moments to smother her emotions, then stepped from the car. Without waiting for her, Burt joined Gordon on the veranda. Irritably Gordon waved towards chairs and said, 'Sit.'

They sat.

'Right,' Gordon started, 'when did you last see Silvio?'

They exchanged all they knew, which wasn't much. Finally, Burt said, 'Where do we go from 'ere?'

'Police?' Gisella said tentatively.

'No!'

'No!'

Gordon and Burt spoke adamantly.

'Why not? Our children are missing, we must do something!'

'No police!' Burt barked.

'Look, my wife has been killed ...' Gordon began.

Burt and Gisella exchanged horrified looks. They guiltily interrupted him, speaking over each other, 'Accept our condolences ... Very sorry for your loss ...' They couldn't believe they had so easily forgotten that terrible fact.

'Yes. Thank you,' Gordon said impatiently. 'Now listen. We all agree neither Susannah nor Silvio could have been involved in that—'

Gisella nodded sadly, her eyes filling with tears.

'—but what are the police going to think if we rush off to them with the news we can't locate our children? We'd never have a moment's peace from the questioning and I, for one, have had enough of their attention already—'

Burt nodded vigorously, glaring.

'—So I suggest we just sit quiet for the moment. Anyone from around here asking questions will be told, um ... what?'

The humid morning breeze blew gently into their faces bringing the promise of a warm day, possibly stormy weather in the coming days. For a few seconds, they considered their options.

'Silvio is visiting restaurants lookin' to expand our client base?' Burt suggested.

'Yes, yes, that's good. And Susannah's gone with him to pick up some new horse equipment we're trialling. She had to go so she could learn how to use it and then teach us.'

Both Burt and Gisella were nodding. 'So, they're in Sydney? Yes, that should work ok. Convenient for them to travel together, coming home soon, blah, blah blah.'

'But *when* do we say they will be back?' Gisella asked miserably. She was still deeply worried.

'Look, just don't give those details out. Let's just wait a bit. They both have phones. I'm sure they will be in touch soon. If you hear from Silvio, let me know and I'll do the same if I hear from Susannah. But for God's sake don't go blabbing to people. Don't mention anything unless someone directly asks you.'

'What if the police ask?' Gisella asked anxiously.

'We say what we agreed on!' Gordon snapped impatiently. 'What an unholy mess. Do you think those two kids know something and they've gone away rather than risk being questioned? Did Silvio say anything? Do you two know anything? Very inconvenient me being in Perth.'

'Everything seemed to be ok up here, although we probably wouldn't have heard if there was trouble. Felicity would have dealt with it herself. But we never heard of any trouble.'

Gisella had been quietly thinking. Her romantic ideas were never far from the front of her mind. She spoke tentatively, 'Maybe they just two young kids in love. Eyes only for each other. Maybe they just take off to be together. Selfish kids. Take advantage of us being distracted. Not think we be worried sick.'

'Sounds stupid to me,' Burt growled.

'No, wait. She might have a point. Maybe we're reading too much into it, with all this other stress. Yes, the more I think of it, the more I think Gisella could be right.'

'Those two must 'ave been pretty damned secretive. I never had a sniff of it. They must 'ave been doing a lot of careful sneakin' around,' Burt still sounded doubtful.

Gordon stood up. 'It wouldn't be hard. It's not as if either of them had to stick to a rigid work timetable. Would we have noticed if they'd been sneaking off? Look, what's done is done. We've sorted out a reasonable story for their absence. We'll deal with the whole relationship thing when they get home. We'll hear from them soon. You both just remember to stick to our agreed story, no matter who asks.'

Despite his own serious misgivings about the situation, his decisive manner went a long way to easing Burt and Gisella's worries. They accepted his words and stood to go.

'Ah Gordon,' Burt began hesitantly, 'sorry we never said anything before. We're real sad about Felicity. If we can do anything to help, let us know. Do you know anythin' about when you can 'ave a funeral?'

'Thanks, Burt.' Gordon's assured manner faltered a bit. 'We have to fit in with whatever the police want, and they said they still have some tests to do. We'll just carry on. Remember, if you hear anything, let me know. Speak to me, don't leave messages.'

With a sketchy wave, Burt shepherded Gisella back to the car. They drove slowly home to a late breakfast neither had much appetite for.

Gordon, frowning heavily, watched them go. He went into the kitchen and made a coffee which he took across to his office on the opposite side of the house. Susannah and Silvio in a relationship? Preposterous! Where can those stupid kids have got to? he wondered. More importantly, what have they done to make running away seem the best option? He couldn't accept that they had just run off to be alone together.

Gordon slumped down behind his desk. His office retained some of the charm hinted at on the outside of the homestead. He had resisted Felicity's redecoration drive, arguing that this was his haven, and he should have it the way he wanted. His leather-topped desk was only slightly cluttered with papers because Darren did most of the paperwork for the stud on the computer in an office-cum-sunroom. Gordon found the pale walls restful. He had hung pictures of their most successful horses from the old-fashioned picture rails that circled the walls.

He decided to spend some time regrouping and reviewing. He made some notes for the next morning, first of which was to get in touch with Felicity's solicitor. Strange to say, Gordon really had no idea what the situation was regarding her last will and testament and how she had left her assets. She had said she was going to update her will before she travelled to England. He had agreed it was a good idea and had meant to bring up with her the question of what alterations she had made before she left. He *assumed* she had made the alterations before leaving. Then things had got busy, and she'd gone before he got around to asking her about it. The unplanned hospitalisation on her return to Australia had forced some plan changes which necessitated pushing back his idea of a speedy return to Antonia in Perth. A mere two days after Felicity was out of hospital, he'd flown west. And now she was dead. He'd need some legal advice on exactly how to go on.

They hadn't ever formalised a company as a base for stud operations. It was all still in Felicity's name. They had discussed making a family company but never got round to setting it up. A bad oversight, Gordon realised with a frown.

Felicity owned the stud outright and ran the business using her personal bank account for all expenses. She paid herself, Gordon, Susannah, and Darren each a generous wage. The other stud and property staff received award wages. Gordon's pay went into his personal bank account, and he used those funds for his travel and other expenses. Susannah and Darren were comfortably off because their wages were bolstered by bequests from their grandfather. Plus, they lived at home and had few other living expenses. Gordon was acutely aware that his habitual self-indulgent spending left him with very little to fall back on in a crisis. Not to mention the expense of flying back and forth to Perth and the motels. He'd had to use some of his own money digging Linda out of her scrape, too. *Might have to tighten my belt.* It was too soon to be raking money in off the top of the scheme he had devised for himself and Linda in Perth.

Gordon expected the solicitors and Felicity's executor would allow continued spending on running the stud. He assumed he would be named executor. He *hoped* that would be the case because if his bank account had to support the stud until probate was cleared, Divine Hayfields would rapidly grind to a halt. He groaned, *How have I taken my eye so far off the ball to have no idea about these things? Felicity was always very capable with managing finances and the stud came to her with her father's fortune, so there shouldn't be a problem.* Felicity also enjoyed her independence and was often reluctant to share financial details with Gordon. He had not minded too much about that, just so long as he had his generous salary and she agreed to his suggested spending. She usually did go along with his ideas because despite enjoying her autonomy, she recognised and bowed to his good judgement.

But Gordon realised he could have some serious problems if he wasn't named as her successor.

He heard movement in the kitchen and yelled, 'Is that you, Darren? I'm in the office.'

Darren, carrying a steaming mug, strolled in wearing his habitual brightly patterned robe. Gordon winced and gently closed his eyes. He silently reminded himself now was not the time to upset Darren with criticism over his taste in robes. He needed all the allies he could muster. With Felicity dead and Susannah, who knows where, his support group was somewhat depleted.

'When did you last see Susannah?' he began.

'Last night when we came home,' Darren said cautiously, aware that the conversation could head into difficult ground, ground he was very keen to avoid.

'Did she say anything to you?'

'Not much, just she was tired and going to bed. I said I was having a drink, but she said she wouldn't join me and that was pretty much it. Why?'

Tiredly, Gordon went through the details of his exchange with Burt and Gisella.

'Can you add anything to that?' he asked.

'Nothing, I'm afraid. Aren't they here somewhere?'

'It appears not. Susannah's car isn't here. I had a quick glance round her room, but nothing obvious is missing ...'

'Hang on, Dad, I'll tell you if she meant to be away or not.' Darren went to Susannah's room and a quick glance confirmed she had packed with deliberation and care.

'Yeah, she meant to be away,' he said confidently.

'How can you tell?' Gordon was disbelieving.

'She's taken her phone charger. Don't worry. Just call her.'

'I've tried but it goes to message.'

'She'll turn it on soon, can't go long without looking at it for something or other.'

'Lucky you know what you're talking about. I wouldn't have thought to look for the damned charger!'

'What's going to happen here, Dad? I mean to the farm and everything. I can't really take anything in or make sense of everything. And did I hear someone say Ali Hadji is missing? Do you think he did this to Mum?'

'No, I don't think so because now the police are talking about poison, saying the fork was stabbed in after she was dead.' Although he spoke matter-of-factly, Gordon felt very squeamish about the details.

'God! How bloody terrible. I wish the stupid cops would get a move on!'

'Be careful what you wish for, son.'

'What do you mean?'

'The questioning is going to get much more intense and persistent. You might need to bear that in mind, if you have any secrets you'd rather not have out in the open,' Gordon said dryly.

Darren blushed. 'Yes of course,' he mumbled. He was suddenly anxious to end the discussion with his father. 'Have you had breakfast?' he asked.

'No. Knock us up some bacon and eggs, will you. It's almost late enough to be lunch!' At the mention of food, Gordon realised he was hungry. His felt his mind sharpen. *I wonder why Ali Hadji has scarpered. I thought he seemed all right. What the heck was going on while I was in Perth,* he mused. *Wait a minute, we must have a phone number for him and his parents. Should I try to track him down, or leave it to the police?* He scribbled a reminder to look into Ali in more detail on Monday, then followed the smell of frying bacon into the kitchen.

CHAPTER FIFTEEN

Susannah opened her eyes and was momentarily puzzled by the unfamiliar room. Then she remembered, and with a happy smile she rolled over to watch Silvio as he slept. This was perfect! They had found this motel yesterday afternoon, dumped their stuff and gone straight down to Town Beach. They'd walked, scuffing their bare toes in the sand, flicking flat pebbles to skip on the water, picking up the odd tiny shell. The salt breeze seemed to blow away all the cobwebs, leaving them feeling already refreshed. With the appetites of youth, they enjoyed a fish and chip supper and a few beers at one of the waterfront pubs, then strolled hand in hand back to the motel. *Oh man! If this is living together*, Susannah thought, *it is picture perfect so far.*

She slid gently out of bed to avoid waking Silvio and eased quietly onto the balcony. The sun was already above a bank of stormy-looking cloud out to sea and the humid coastal air wafted round her. With a contented sigh she relaxed into the curve of the deck chair and closed her eyes.

Warm hands smoothing softly over her shoulders roused her from her doze and she looked up into Silvio's deep brown eyes, raising her face for a long kiss.

Over breakfast a while later, they discussed their situation. Susannah was so delighted with the relaxation and freedom from sneaking around and the absence of police, she was reluctant to do anything other than enjoy it all. Silvio, on the other hand, was aware of a growing sense of responsibility mixed with strong feelings of protectiveness for his girl. He wanted her to enjoy all the relaxing benefits this holiday offered but he knew their parents would now be seriously worried by their absence. He suggested they make calls home, gently reminding Susannah that her father was already dealing with the death of her mother and really didn't need the extra worry of a missing daughter. She guiltily agreed but pleaded that they just enjoy themselves for a little while longer. While they discussed it, Susannah let her imagination drift to the prospect of having Gisella for a mother-in-law and realised linking her life to Silvio's would not be all plain sailing. She shrugged ruefully and grinned, reflecting that she'd be living with Silvio, not his mum. While they ate, Susannah eyed the billowing storm clouds that had by now obliterated the sun and idly wondered what was forecast in the weather.

Neither of them had watched or read any news since arriving at the coast. They had no idea a strong storm front was approaching and that there were weather alerts all up and down the coast for heavy rain, damaging winds and flooding. They really should have been heading inland while they could but at this stage, ignorance was bliss. They didn't notice that the tourist numbers seemed somewhat lower than yesterday.

Silvio laid his knife and fork on his empty plate and sighed with enjoyment. Susannah kissed him happily and said, 'Come on then, let's cut loose and have ourselves a holiday!'

They spent a leisurely morning window-shopping through the many enticing shops in the main street. While they lunched, they decided on a dolphin watching cruise, since the overcast weather made the beach unappealing. At the waterfront, they booked onto a two-hour cruise. The cruise operator warned everyone that if the weather came in, the cruise would be cut short, but he reassured them all that if that happened, there would be refunds. Silvio privately thought they would be lucky to see a dolphin, but Susannah clutched his arm excitedly and dragged him to seats close to the front of the boat. He turned his face into the wind, surprised to notice it was much stronger than earlier.

Back at Divine Hayfields, life on the surface went on as normal. Kevin was working with Divine Madam while Jarred had the lads carrying out all the duties that demanded attention on every horse stud. They had a full load thanks to the absences of Susannah, Ali and Hamish, not to mention Mrs Hathaway. Jarred was pleased that the lack of manpower left little time for gossip. He had admired Mrs Hathaway and felt that idle chatter was disrespectful. Darren was at his computer, absent-mindedly carrying out routine updates in the stud records. Fortunately, his tasks didn't require much thought as his mind kept drifting to his lover, his mother, her murderer, his future, anything but work.

Gordon was in his office. He'd realised the time difference meant he wouldn't be able to try to contact Ali until later in the day. He was waiting for Felicity's solicitor to return his call. Crumden, Crumden and Hollis had offices in Muswellbrook and Felicity had chosen to use them for convenience because her father had used them. She liked their familiarity with the stud and its workings. They often gave her guiding advice before she asked for it which she greatly appreciated. It was not in her nature to appear inept or at a loss and their prompts and guidelines in the right direction certainly helped her appear competent and in control. It wasn't as if she didn't know what she was doing but their quiet advice behind the scenes bolstered her confidence. Gordon used a firm in Scone for his personal needs. He doodled idly while he waited, wondering how soon he could get back to Perth and Antonia. *God, I miss her!* He jumped when the phone warbled beside him.

The conversation with Mr Crumden was brief, and at the end of the call Gordon sat in puzzled silence. He frowned as he processed the gist of the minimal information he had received. He was no further ahead at all. The solicitor had refused to reveal the contents of Felicity's will, insisting that Gordon come to his offices that afternoon. He had further insisted that Gordon arrange for Mac Brennan to attend the offices with him. Gordon could not fathom any reason for Mac Brennan to be involved.

He headed to the stables in search of Mac.

'Hey, Jarred, how's it going?' Gordon walked down through the tack room door, running his eyes approvingly over the clean and orderly equipment.

Jarred looked up from hammering new pegs into the bridle bar. 'Not bad, Boss. Any news?'

For a second, Gordon stiffened, thinking Jarred was referring to Susannah's absence. Then he realised Jarred's question related to the ongoing police enquiry.

'No, mate. I guess these things take time. D'you have any idea where I might find Mac? And can you spare him this afternoon?'

Jarred's heart sank at the thought of losing yet another pair of hands, but he couldn't very well argue with his boss. 'Jason has just mulched the two top paddocks and he and Mac are shifting the yearlings up there. They shouldn't be long. I was going to ask Mac to school a couple of the older horses this afternoon. But that can wait.' Jarred stifled the urge to ask why the Boss wanted Mac, knowing the reason would be given if Gordon wanted to give it.

'Thanks,' Gordon said and turned to go, almost colliding with Mac at the door.

'Ah, just who I was looking for. I need to see the solicitor in town later and they want to see you too. Meet me at the house at two o'clock and you can come in my car, save you petrol.'

Jarred, watching with interest from within the shed, saw Mac's face turn from polite to doubtful to pale and horrified.

He stammered and stuttered, finally managing to splutter out that he'd take his own car, thanks, so he could go straight home after the appointment. 'Got to get on,' he mumbled, spinning on his heel, and rapidly departing.

'What the hell?' Gordon grated irritably.

Jarred hesitated to answer, hoping that Gordon would leave without further involving him.

'What's his problem?'

'Well Boss. I couldn't say. He's normally easy-going, but pretty quiet. Maybe things have just got to him. It's been a bit of a strain on them all, not knowing who, ah, attacked Mrs Hathaway.'

'Yes, of course, that will be it. Right, well, you carry on and remember, Mac and I will be in town this afternoon.' Jarred allowed himself a frustrated sigh. As if he was likely to forget he would be yet another man short this afternoon! Gordon strode back towards the house, mulling over Mac's extraordinary reaction.

Mac almost ran to the quad bike and quickly headed back to the top paddock. He stopped where he had a good all-round view to see anyone coming and took out his mobile phone. He pressed the familiar sequence of numbers and waited impatiently for an answer.

'Yeah, it's me. Oh God! Gordon just told me to go to the solicitors' with him this afternoon. I'm not ready for this. It's going to be bloody awful!'

'Sweetheart, you've done nothing wrong. He can't hurt you. You didn't look for any of this. You've done what was asked of you. Take a breath. Really, it'll probably be better once it's all out in the open. Relax, you'll be fine. I'll take the afternoon off so I can be at home when you get there. Come on, love, calm down, it'll be ok.'

'You're right. Just shocked me because I don't want to deal with it. I guess I should have realised this would happen sooner rather than later.'

'Of course. But Felicity's death has been a big blow. It's understandable not to have thought any further than that. Stop worrying and I'll see you at home later.'

'Ok love, as usual you've helped me back on track. Dunno where I'd be without you. Thanks, love. Later.'

Mac relaxed onto the seat of the quad bike and breathed deeply trying to clear his head and take his wife's advice. He massaged his temples with his fingertips then let his eyes run over the calming rural scene below. With a deep sigh, he started the bike and returned to Jarred for instructions for the rest of his day. Or at least until he had to see the solicitor.

In town, Kaylee and Ben were reviewing their accumulated information. It was now clear that Felicity was poisoned and died from the poisoning before the pitchfork was thrust in her back. The poison was proving difficult to identify. It seemed possible the poison was added to the sedatives or the blood clot treatment.

'We got a clear print off that plant pot that I was whacked with but there aren't any matches on the database. Guess that means we'll have to go and get prints from everyone. What a drag,' Ben said.

'Well let's go and do that now, so we can be back here in time for you to try and locate Ali in big old non-English speaking Syria,' Kaylee teased Ben a little to lighten his mood.

'Oh, didn't I mention, I found an Arabic speaker who can help?'

Ben's casual words stunned Kaylee. She had been looking forward to watching him struggle to find Ali dealing with people whose language he didn't speak. Ben grinned wickedly. 'Yeah. Guy works for the contractors who clean all the schools, comes from Damascus. Very handy, don't you think?'

'How did you find him?' Kaylee was quite irritated that Ben had managed to dig up an interpreter in such a short time.

'I have my contacts,' Ben chortled. 'Let's go.'

They drove in silence while Kaylee consoled herself that how Ben got onto an Arabic speaker was not important. It would be a huge leap forward if they could locate Ali Hadji and decide whether he had anything to do with Mrs Hathaway's death.

'We'd better stop at Bunrack's farm first and get their prints,' she finally said.

They drove in between the ornate lion pillars and spotted Burt working in the market gardens that stretched away to the left of the house. He straightened at the sound of the vehicle and his shoulders drooped as he resigned himself to more difficult conversations with the police.

Gisella answered their knock and as before they gathered in the sunroom. Ben was immediately aware that Gisella and Burt were more wary than before. Gisella's eyes were flicking constantly to Burt. He wouldn't make eye contact with her, and his mouth was shut in a thin grim line. *Probably another fight,* Ben mused, but he felt there could have been more to it than just their regular volatility.

'We won't be taking up too much of your time,' Kaylee opened casually, 'we just need to take your fingerprints. We need to be sure you are not connected with a piece of evidence we've collected.'

Gisella jumped and gripped the edge of the table. Burt made a gesture of impatience. 'Well get on with it then!'

'We need Silvio's prints too,' Ben said, 'Is he about?' He was watching Gisella carefully and noted her pale face and her large tense eyes.

Neither of the Bunracks spoke for a moment, then they jumped in together, paused and faltered to a stop.

Kaylee tried the persuasive approach. 'Can you get Silvio for us, Burt?'

'No!' he said shortly. 'He's not 'ere.'

This is like pulling teeth, Ben groaned inwardly.

There was silence for a moment.

'He's in Sydney. Looking for new clients. Be back few days,' Gisella said shrilly and rapidly. Burt glared at her. She shrugged and turned away from him.

'In Sydney? I thought we asked that nobody leave the area without talking to us,' Ben said mildly.

'Can't be 'elped. Arrangements were made. We can't put our business on 'old while you lot muck about at your own casual pace. We 'ave to make a living you know,' Burt snapped. 'Take our prints and we'll send Silvio in when he gets home.'

'Where's he staying? We need to be able to get onto him.'

Burt jumped in before Gisella could open her mouth. 'Gisella's aunt Celeste.'

'Her name and contact details, please, now!' Ben snapped. He was tired of all the lying.

Gisella looked appealingly at Burt. He nodded impatiently. Face pale and fingers shaking, Gisella, opened her phone and quickly recited her aunt's name and contact details.

'When will he be home?'

'Not sure, not long, coupla days.'

The prints collected, Kaylee and Ben continued to Divine Hayfields. They were both silently going over their visit to Croham, pondering the excessive tension at the house and minimal explanation of Silvio's absence. Kaylee voiced Ben's thought when she commented that the lack of information from the Bunracks could be their way to conceal some vital truth.

Gisella threw herself into a chair and burst into loud sobs.

'Shh, love. Stop. Pull y'self together. We'll just ring Celeste and explain. Tell her to tell the cops Silvio has gone to stay with friends. That might hold them off 'til Silvio gets home. Dratted boy has caused a packet of trouble going off with Susannah like that.'

As usual, any criticism of her son diverted Gisella, and she took refuge in daydreaming about him and Susannah.

After fingerprinting everyone at Divine Highfields, the detectives had even more to contemplate. Susannah's absence had been explained by her father with the same curt lack of detail that Burt had used.

'Who is Susannah staying with?' Ben rapped.

Blandly Gordon said, 'She and Silvio are at his cousin's place.'

'Cousin? Do you have a name?'

'Ah, no. It was just convenient for Susannah to go with Silvio and pick up our equipment. So, we organised for them to stay there. Short notice, you know. Easier than messing about with motels.'

'Right! Be so kind as to give us Susannah's number, *now.*' She decided if these people would not be helpful, she would use police resources to locate Susannah and either prove or disprove what they were being told. She was tired of getting nowhere because of lies and misinformation. What was the problem with these people?

Gordon half-heartedly gave Susannah's number. He didn't think the police would have any more success than he had getting in touch with Susannah, but he knew his lies would look bad if they *did* speak to her!

'What a crock!' Kaylee exploded when they were in the car. Were Susannah and Silvio even in Sydney? Was it really a planned expedition? What details were being concealed and why? Surely those two couldn't be involved in Mrs Hathaway's murder.

'I'll be using triangulation on Susannah's phone while you're looking for Ali. I've been messed about too much now! They had their chance to be honest and they blew it.'

'If too many more people leave the area, we'll have nobody left to investigate,' Ben said gloomily as they returned to the police station.

'Don't you worry, Ben. I'll find Susannah and Silvio will be with her. By the way, Darren wasn't happy to give us his prints, was he,' Kaylee snapped. 'Do you think *he* had something to do with his mother's death as well?'

'Who would know? Fair dinkum, this is the most unproductive investigation I've ever been involved in!' Ben retorted, giving vent to his frustration.

'Hey, steady on! Two of the best are on the case. What's with all the discouragement?' Kaylee put the lid on her frustration and spoke lightly, trying to get him to ease up. Two frustrated detectives led to mistakes being made and they couldn't afford that with this slow-moving investigation. 'You know cases all have their dead spots. The pace will pick up soon.'

'Yeah, right,' Ben growled.

Clicks strolled into the office, smiling widely. 'We've got the poison! Took a bit of doing, but we're sure now.'

Two pairs of eyes fixed on Clicks' smug smile. 'Well?' Ben demanded.

'Ricin! Sourced from the castor oil plant which is fairly common round here. It's on the NSW weeds list and most people voluntarily get rid of it because its toxic to humans and animals. Here, look at a picture of the plant. Did you notice any growing at Divine Hayfields?'

'No, but I don't usually pay much attention to plants,' Kaylee admitted.

'It often grows in gullies and waterways,' Clicks began.

'You're a mine of information, you little gem!' Ben cut in excitedly. 'That wetland Burt was going on about, Kaylee, remember? We need to take a look at it! They had a temporary fence round it, so it hasn't been grazed. Anything could be growing there.'

'Hang on just a second, Ben,' Clicks said sharply. 'If you're thinking of collecting some, just remember that plant is poisonous. Make sure you wear gloves and don't rub your eyes or touch your skin. Be very careful.'

'Thanks for the warning. Coming Boss? I bet we find some castor oil plants there.'

'Yeah,' Kaylee said slowly. 'Clicks, have you got any ideas how the ricin was administered? In the sedatives? On the anti-clotting needle? If it was in either of those, it narrows the suspect list down to someone who had easy access to Mrs Hathaway's bedroom. And that would be Susannah, Darren and Gordon Hathaway. At a pinch, the housekeeper, what was her name? Delia? No. Dell! Dell Sullivan. But, unless it was Ali Hadji, Hamish or Silvio, and that's why they've run away, then the Hathaways and Dell Sullivan are the only people who could be responsible. Maybe Susannah and Darren worked together. Maybe Silvio and Susannah worked together.' Kaylee felt rejuvenated, her mind spinning over possibilities. She thought a little longer.

'Ben, I don't think you need to come with me to look for weeds. I want you to stay here and use your cleverly sourced translator to get onto Ali. We need to crank this up. Before I go on a weed hunt, I'll get the techs onto triangulating Susannah's phone. If you have any luck with Ali, we should know what he's been up to and where Susannah and Silvio are before the end of the day.'

'Get a sample of the weeds you find, so we can verify that the castor oil plant is readily available out there. But like I said, be careful. We're fairly sure the anti-clotting needles were tampered with,' Clicks said.

'Ok, thanks. That's great work, Clicks.' With a brief wave, Kaylee briskly went on her way.

CHAPTER SIXTEEN

The approaching bad weather had put many of the tourists remaining in town off the dolphin cruise, so there were only five other passengers with Susannah and Silvio. Two were obviously a retired couple who both seemed to suffer with arthritic hips and legs. Their movements were slow and unsteady. A young blond man lounged his long slim body across two seats. He greeted the cruise guide with a familiar, 'Hey, Sam'.

Sam nodded, 'Hey, Shorty.'

The other couple appeared to be a mother and daughter. The girl looked to be in her teens and Susannah idly thought she should have been at school.

Sam, cruise guide as well as skipper, deftly fastened the chain across the opening once they had all stepped aboard. He steered the little boat across the growing waves. The wind buffeted their faces and made streamers of their hair. Silvio looked back, noting how quickly they had already motored far out to sea. He sensed they were heading northeast, although he couldn't see any land to use as a reference point and the sun had been obscured for hours. The clouds billowed and changed; their darkness reflected on the gunmetal foam-tipped water. He wondered, *Was it a mistake getting on the boat? Wouldn't dolphins be hiding in calmer sheltered waters in weather like this?* He put his arm round Susannah's shoulder, feeling her shiver a little. Raindrops suddenly hissed down, passing in windblown sheets. They shifted into the centre of the boat to escape the worst of the slanting rain under the canopy roof and pressed together for reassurance and warmth. *The rain must have made the temperature drop about ten degrees,* Silvio thought. The wind increased and the boat tossed roughly. Sam was beginning to look concerned and belatedly decided to hand out life jackets.

'He should have done that when we got on the boat,' Silvio muttered in Susannah's ear.

'Oh well, better late than never,' she replied trying to sound matter of fact. She slipped her hand into his, glad of his protective arm around her. She was a level-headed person, not given to tears and hysteria but Silvio's presence bolstered her courage.

A snapping flash of lightening and a loud thunderclap made everyone jump. The rain increased to relentless grey sheets. The boat pitched on the choppy waves. Everyone held their seat or each other to avoid being thrown about. The canopy was useless protection against the driving rain. The group were quickly drenched and cold.

Without even a warning splutter, the outboard motor cut out, leaving the boat wallowing. It bounced around on the waves, rocking on the crests, and thudding down into the troughs. They made slow, terrifying headway, completely at the mercy of the howling wind.

Shorty offered to try to steer the powerless boat so Sam

could check out the motor. He pulled the starter rope again and again, but the engine stayed lifeless. He was half blinded by the rain, peering at the fuel lines. Suddenly he straightened up and shouted, 'The fuel line has split! We've lost all the fuel.'

He went back up to take over the wheel, more for reassurance than for any steering effect. The teenage girl was clinging to her mother, crying. The two older passengers held onto each other. They slid back and forth on their bench seat. Silvio held Susannah tight while she stared grim-faced at the violent storm.

'Put your bag strap over your head under your life vest, sweetheart, so you don't lose it even if you let it go,' Silvio advised Susannah, then raised his voice and repeated his advice for everyone. He added, 'Men, put your phones and wallets in zip pockets of your life vest.'

Sam tried using the radio to call for help but all he got was static. Either the radio was broken as well as the fuel lines or the storm was causing too much interference. The unremitting rain slashed their bodies. Shorty helped the older couple onto seats beside the mother and daughter. He checked their life jackets were correctly fitted. He moved back up to Sam, gripping the rail as he went.

'What's your plan, man?'

'With no radio and no engine, I don't have much of a plan,' Sam replied. 'Have you got phone signal?'

Shorty checked. 'No, mate. What about your EPIRB?' (Emergency Position-Indicating Radio Beacon)

'Yeah, activated that when the motor stopped. Doubt if anyone will be able to do much about it in this, anyway.

Bloody hell, it came in a bit faster than I expected and I checked every ten minutes before we left. Do me a favour, mate, and keep an eye on the old couple. The others look ok but those two don't look very strong.'

'Got it.'

Sam looked at the compass. 'We're being blown pretty much north, northwest. We'll probably hit the coast somewhere between Port and Crescent Head. Damn! What a mess! Only thing we can really do is hope she stays upright. I don't like our chances if she capsizes.'

Although he'd tried not to speak too loudly, Susannah overheard Sam's last comments. She clung to Silvio.

'Oh no! We can't capsize out here! We *have* to make the coast. It's our only hope.'

'Shh, sweetheart. We'll be ok. Don't panic or it'll upset the others. We can't be too far out to sea. Maybe the clouds are just blocking our view of land,' he reassured her.

Susannah realised the sense of Silvio's words. She stiffened her back and resolved to be calm and as helpful to the others as she could be if disaster struck. Not that disaster hadn't already struck, she supposed, but things could definitely get worse. *Oh boy,* she thought, *nothing like a crisis to show your true colours to your new love! I'll be strong,* she vowed silently. *I want Silvio to be proud of me, to know he can rely on me through good and bad.*

Silvio was having much the same thoughts. Up to now, he had allowed his parents to take care of every difficulty he encountered. He grimly decided now was the time to show what he was made of. He was very nervous, but his pride would not allow him to appear at a disadvantage next to Sam and Shorty. *So, what if I lack their obvious practical experience? I am intelligent, have common sense and can learn fast.* He also had an over-riding desire to protect and care for Susannah. He believed they had a great future together and he wanted it to begin as soon as possible.

* * *

Gordon drove to his appointment, half listening to the radio. The wind was picking up and sheets of rain crossed the windscreen. Branches and leaves were already scattered over the road. His attention sharpened when a weather warning advised of heavy rain associated with extreme weather on the coast. He wished he had a clear idea where Susannah and Silvio were. He had an inkling they had gone off together to escape the stress and tension at home. He envied them their irresponsible impulsiveness. He made a mental note to try to call Susannah again when he stopped in town.

He pulled up at the solicitor's offices and dialled Susannah's number only to receive the notification that the phone was out of range. *At least that will stop the damned cops getting on to her,* he thought grimly. He rang Burt and asked if he any fresh news as to where Silvio and Susannah were. He wasn't surprised to hear Burt knew nothing. He asked Burt to try Silvio's number to find out where they were and disconnected. Moments later, Burt rang to say that he'd been unable to get Silvio on the phone. Gordon cursed inwardly, and with a growing sense of unease, ran through the now steady rain to Mr Crumden's reception to wait for Mac.

Mac's forbidding face when he arrived didn't do anything to allay Gordon's nervousness. He was completely at a loss to explain Mac's presence.

At the police station. Kaylee tracked down one of the technical team. She gave him Susannah's phone number and explained that it was now urgent that she find the phone owner.

'Use all your skill and all the technology available to you. These people have lied and lied to me. I refuse to be taken for a fool and I want to see their faces when I say I've located this woman!' She was methodical in her policing, but she had reached the end of her patience with the lies and deception in this investigation. 'Phone me as soon as you get some results, please. Where this phone has been in the last thirty-six hours should cover it.'

'Sure thing,' the assurance came. Like all technical operators, he relished challenges such as this.

'Thanks.' With a wave, Kaylee grabbed her keys and left in search of weeds.

Mr Crumden's door opened, and he beckoned Gordon and Mac, gesturing towards seats on the other side of his desk.

He began by offering his condolences to both men. Why Mac? Gordon was puzzled. Then the solicitor detailed the legal reasons for his current course of action, meticulously preparing the way for his next words.

All quite boring. Get on with it, Gordon fumed silently. Mac sat rigidly still in his chair, looking intently at the solicitor.

'If the police request it, I shall furnish them with a copy

of this will,' Mr Crumden's dry voice droned on, while he carefully spread out the will on his desk.

He started reading. Gordon barely took in the gist. He had ears only for the word "bequeath".

The monologue continued. '—Bequeath the Divine Hayfields portion of the estate of the below signed Felicity Hathaway in its entirety to—'

Gordon straightened. Mac's face paled.

'—my first-born son, Macalister Wheeler Brennan of 3 Main Street, Wheeler.'

'WHAT?' Gordon leapt to his feet, knocking over his chair. 'What nonsense is this?' he roared.

'Please sit down, Mr Hathaway,' the solicitor said sharply. 'We have not finished.'

'How is Mac involved?' demanded Gordon. He was shaking, groping to set the chair right.

He sat down, glaring at Mac. 'Did you know about this, you snake?' he growled at Mac.

Mac sat white-faced, not meeting Gordon's eye. He fixed his attention steadfastly on Mr Crumden.

'Shall I explain, this to Gordon, Mac? Or would you prefer to do it?' Mr Crumden politely asked Mac.

'You, please,' Mac replied in a strained voice.

'Well, Gordon, a short history for you. When she was 17, Felicity ran away from her boarding school due to a temporary infatuation with a member of staff of the business that supplied foodstuffs to the school.'

Gordon fell back into his seat with his hand on his mouth, eyes wide and aghast. 'She had a son before I married her?' he murmured in shocked disbelief.

Mr Crumden continued calmly, 'She and the staff member were not located until some ten days after their flight. They were found in a holiday flat on the south coast. Felicity was expelled from the school. Before she could be re-enrolled at another school, it was discovered she was pregnant. Her education was completed by a private tutor at Divine Hayfields or Wheeler Park as it was known then. The relative isolation of the property enabled Felicity to carry the pregnancy to full term away from gossips and prying eyes.'

Gordon felt sick. He felt he had handled the news of Felicity's death with the correct amount of grace and dignity. He had held it together in the face of the police questioning. He had maintained a calm and positive face dealing with everything since returning from Perth. But this news was threatening to undermine everything! It felt as if he was grasping sand to stop himself sliding downhill. He was close to panic.

The solicitor paused for a beat, then carried on his narrative. 'Felicity's father knew of a couple in the village who were desperately trying to have a child. He met with them and completed an agreement where they would raise the baby as their own. The couple, Mr and Mrs Brennan, were overjoyed. Mr Wheeler agreed to be responsible for all costs involved in raising the child, including education at a private school. In exchange, Mr and Mrs Brennan were not to reveal where the child came from. In due course, Mac was born. It was left to Mr and Mrs Brannan to choose whether to let Mac know he was, in fact, adopted. They opted to tell Mac about his adoption and who his mother was. They impressed on him the need for silence about his birth mother's identity. When Mac turned eighteen, Felicity met him at Brennan's home. She asked him to continue to keep her secret. She promised him employment on the stud should he ever wish to work in a rural setting. Mac had attended an agriculture college and being interested in rural work said he would remember her offer. Over the next few years, they developed a comfortable relationship. Mac travelled to Queensland gathering experience working on various properties. A few years later he returned to the Hunter Valley and contacted Felicity to take up her offer of employment. By then he was married, and he wanted to give his wife the stability of permanent employment.'

While Mr Crumden continued to enlighten Gordon with a tale Mac was already familiar with, he took time to process the information Mr Crumden had shared. What had possessed his mother to leave the whole of Divine Hayfields to him? Susannah and Darren would be no more pleased than Gordon was! What a mess. Although he was horrified to be the recipient of such a massive asset, part of him was already grappling with ideas he could put to work to further develop the asset. Excitement warred with panic at the future he glimpsed. Gordon's next words yanked him back to the present.

'You're really her *son*?' Gordon was floundering. He went on the attack: 'What about your father? This delivery boy?' he sneered.

Mac drew a deep breath. 'Gordon,' he said firmly, 'You won't hurt me by disparaging my natural father. He and I have a secure relationship. I had the same with Felicity, as I have with my adopted parents in Wheeler. They are proud grandparents to my son. Felicity was a doting grandparent, as is my natural father. My son is fortunate to have so many loving role models. We have all been devastated by Felicity's death. I did not know this was how Felicity intended to leave her estate. Until now, I respected Felicity's wishes to keep our relationship quiet. I realised the story of my birth would come out when her will was read. I do not want my son or my wife subject to any slurs or unpleasantness from you now that you know Felicity had a son before she married you.'

'I'll contest the bloody will! This is preposterous. What about *my* children with Felicity? Is it fair that they miss out because of you?'

Mr Crumden cut in. 'Felicity has made some monetary bequests which we will come to in a moment. You'll remember the rather large bequests Mr Wheeler left Susannah and Darren. Those were intended in part to cushion Susannah's and Darren's prospects, no matter how Felicity disposed of Divine Hayfields in the future. He was a far-sighted old man, was Mr Wheeler.' A note of nostalgia crept into Mr Crumden's dry voice.

'Well, these bequests had better be substantial,' blustered Gordon. He anxiously hoped he, too, would receive a generous consideration. If he didn't, a very different future was revealing itself to him and he was shocked by the implications. *Thank God for Antonia,* he thought. He desperately tried to find some bright spots in what had suddenly become a very bleak outlook.

Although he had been educated at a private school,

Gordon had attended on a scholarship. His mother had married a migrant labourer when she was very young. She had been widowed when his sister was three and he was a baby. Her life was a constant struggle to provide the basics for herself and her young family. Gordon used all the benefits of his education and the contacts he made while at school to the best advantage he could. He disliked revealing his impoverished origins. Instead of being proud of his mother's devotion in striving to give him the best she could, in most instances he never mentioned her or his background. As a young man, he ruthlessly pursued wealthy peers to befriend. He had made sure to introduce his sister to all his well-off friends, aware that if Linda didn't marry into money, he would have to support her. When he met Felicity, her vivacity had entranced him but the underlying attraction to her was that in answer to all his discrete questions, the answer came loudly back: 'Money, money, money'.

The marriage had worked reasonably well, despite Felicity's volatility. Gordon recognised the financial security of life with Felicity and that was a powerful incentive to be a peacekeeper. Together they had enjoyed their position as successful horse breeders. He realised that in recent years, they had become accustomed to pursuing their own interests and not sharing as much as previously. The fact that she had apparently effortlessly concealed her relationship with Mac, the fact that she had been cooing over a grandchild he knew nothing about, the fact that she had so easily slipped Mac onto the payroll made Gordon realise what a chasm had opened between them. He, too, had rather casually fallen into the relationship with Antonia. It was only in recent months he had begun to see Antonia in a more mercenary light. He had reverted easily to his former habit of making alliances only with people who could help him financially or socially or both.

Gordon belatedly realised he had made a massive mistake when he failed to check with Felicity about the details of her will. He winced at the immense stupidity of his very basic error. He silently berated himself for letting his attention wander to a possible future in Perth instead of keeping if firmly fixed on his current situation at Divine Hayfields. He had felt very secure being married to Felicity and her money despite their regular disagreements. He enjoyed being well-off, well-known, and influential in his local community. He had cold-bloodedly made plans to painlessly extricate himself from his marriage. He had allowed himself to be beguiled by the prospect of future wealth from his Perth scheme. He had even occasionally allowed himself to imagine a smooth transfer from Felicity and the Hunter Valley to Antonia and Perth. He knew Antonia was very well respected in business circles in Perth and he imagined she had many influential friends he could get to know.

His plans would crumble to dust, if there was no financial gain for him in Felicity's will. He was shattered.

'Let us continue, Gordon. Keep your interruptions to the minimum. It is a very detailed testament.' Mr Crumden suppressed a sigh, wondering if they would get through the document before closing time.

A long time later, Mr Crumden concluded the meeting,

advising the men that the farm was to continue to be run as normally as possible and as a profitable venture until such time as probate was granted and the rightful owner could take over.

Both men left the office deeply shrouded in their own very different thoughts. Neither spoke to the other as they went their separate ways.

CHAPTER SEVENTEEN

The driving rain darkened the sky until the late afternoon seemed like evening. Susannah felt as if they had been thrown about and soaked for hours. She peered anxiously towards what she hoped was the coast. Was that land? Was that dark shadow land, or just thicker cloud?

She gripped Silvio's arm. 'Look!' she whispered in his ear, 'Is that land?' He stared into the waves and rain and cloud.

'You're right! I think it is.'

At the same time, Sam pointed excitedly. 'Land!' he shouted.

The coastline showed as a dark line not very far across the lashing seas. Silvio tried to guess the distance. He worried that the coastline looked so dark because it was a rocky area. What hope would any of them have if they were tossed up onto rocks?

Sam and Shorty had a quiet conversation, then beckoned Silvio.

'Look mate,' Sam started, 'We're going to need you and probably your girlfriend. We need strong, level-headed types. There's eight of us. Four strong, four weak.' Silvio opened his mouth to speak.

'Yeah,' cut in Sam, 'I know you want to look after your girlfriend but look at what we've got: an old man, old lady, older woman (I think her name is Mel), teenager (maybe Carla, I think she said), strong young woman and three strong young men. I reckon if we can get the mother of that crying teenager to calm her down, your girlfriend might be able to look after the lass. That would leave the other three for us to manage. Do you reckon that would work?'

Silvio felt a surge of pride as he realised he and Susannah could be helpful. He nodded and beckoned Susannah.

Sam detailed the plan he had in mind. He wanted to be as close to shore as possible before they left the boat. They would fix a bottle of water to each person from the supplies on the boat. The four stronger ones would each be responsible for a weaker person. Everyone would use the swimming skills they had and their life jacket to try to make shore. Susannah nodded decisively and went back to the other passengers. She explained the plan. The older couple looked relieved that they would not be struggling ashore on their own. Sam began handing water bottles to Shorty and Silvio.

Mel, the mother, sensibly started to soothe Carla. She pointed out that Carla could be part of the successful rescue if she pulled herself together and made up her mind to help. Susannah chimed in, 'We are young and strong. It is up to us to use our strength to help those who are weaker. Are you a good swimmer?'

Carla nodded doubtfully. 'Will you be with me, Mum?'

'Look love, you're a much better swimmer than me. I'll

probably need help.' She turned to Susannah, 'We're Mel and Carla. What's your name?'

'I'm Susannah and Carla is in luck. I was on the swimming squad at school.' Susannah gave a confident grin, trying to bolster Carla's courage. 'I know I look a bit older than you, but school wasn't that long ago,' she joked. Carla responded with a watery smile.

Sam told the older man he would help him, and Silvio would help the elderly wife, leaving Shorty to take care of Mel. They each carefully tied bottles of water onto the cords on their life jackets. Susannah made sure the women had securely tucked their handbags inside their life jackets. Sam made sure the men had their mobile phones zipped in the lifejacket pockets. He had attached the second emergency beacon to his life jacket. Susannah glanced around the group. She gave a quick nod. She thought they were as ready as they would ever be. She squinted ashore through the rain and was stunned to see how close the coastline was. *Maybe this rescue is not as impossible as it seems,* she thought.

The rain continued to smash the group huddled on the boat. The wind was screaming and dragging at them, but they could feel the tide drawing the boat to shore.

'We're lucky the tide is carrying us in,' Sam commented. 'The main thing to remember is to get cleanly off the boat,' he shouted above the wind. 'I'm going to open the chain where you stepped on board. If you don't think you can jump off over the side, go out through that opening.'

They could all clearly see the shore now, dark in front of them with rugged rocks. Slightly south of the rocks was dirty sand and wind torn shrubs. 'Try to get to the sandy part of the beach,' Shorty advised.

Susannah gauged the distance. 'Do you reckon you could swim ashore from here, Carla?'

Carla nodded. Susannah looked at Silvio and he squeezed her hand. She smiled and glanced at Sam. He nodded. She took Carla's hand, stood up and said confidently, 'Let's go!'

They landed in the cold choppy water together and Susannah felt Carla start kicking for shore. She swam strongly beside her, nudging her towards the sandy beach. She felt the waves carry her and risked a quick look behind. Silvio and the old lady were in the water. He had opted for the lifesaving carry technique rather than expecting her to swim. Sam was swimming closely beside the old man who seemed to be managing quite well. Mel was bobbing around alone. Susannah scanned the rough water but couldn't see Shorty anywhere.

She shifted her attention ahead. Carla was a little in front of her, still swimming strongly. Suddenly she stood up.

'I'm in shallow water! I can wade ashore,' she yelled with relief. Susannah felt sand under her feet and sagged gratefully. Then she stiffened her shoulders and yelled to Carla, 'Get yourself far up the beach and be prepared to help the others if they need it. I'm going back to help Shorty and your mum.'

Carla hesitated, 'What about Mum?'

'Go!' Susannah yelled forcefully. 'See if you can help the others.'

She turned and headed back into the frothing choppy seas. She swam out, pushing against the tide, passing Sam and the older man swimming steadily in. She checked ahead and could see Mel quite close, floating inshore. She dog paddled for a beat.

'Carla is safe! Keep it up, Mel, you're doing great. Just keep floating,' she yelled with encouragement. 'What happened to Shorty?'

'I don't know. He seemed to be having some sort of attack. I think he's still on the boat.'

Susannah nodded. She glanced round for Silvio. He was strongly ploughing through the water with the old lady. She turned back towards the boat. It was closer to the shore now.

In a few moments, she hauled herself up onto the tossing boat. She glanced round.

Shorty was curled on the floor, groaning in pain.

'Shorty, what's wrong?' She quickly knelt beside him.

'Pain, dreadful, stomach. He groaned between gasps. 'Oh God!'

'Where? Where's the pain? We've got to get off the boat! Its heading for the rocks,' Susannah said.

He groaned and gestured to his abdomen. Susannah thought fast. She figured Shorty would be much safer off the boat no matter what was wrong with him. She realised the swim ashore was much shorter now, but it would be tricky avoiding the rocks.

'Mate, we've got to go! Can you swim? If not, I can do the rescue swim with you. It's not far. Is there a first aid box, do you think?'

Shorty nodded.

'I'll get you some pain med and then we're going. I know it'll be horrid for you but we're safer off the boat.' She ran forward swaying with the rocking vessel. She quickly located the first aid box. She grabbed some pain tablets and a tough plastic bag. She thrust the box into the plastic bag and tied the neck. She grabbed a bottle of water and carried it and the first aid box back to Shorty.

She held out the tablets and the water.

Just then, Sam climbed over the side into the boat.

'Oh, so glad to see YOU!' Susannah said. 'One of us is taking Shorty ashore, the other is taking the first aid box. Which is yours?'

'I'll take Shorty. You take the box. Shorty, we're outta here. Give me a hand to lug him overboard, Susannah. Then get yourself to safety.'

'Right.' She wound the neck of the plastic bag round her hand and jumped back in the water.

It seemed mere seconds before she felt sand under her feet again. She looked back and saw Sam coming with Shorty.

'Susannah!' Silvio was next to her. She quickly explained and pushed him towards the other two men. 'Give them a hand,' she said, and continued up the beach.

Carla and her mum were sheltering under some sparse shrubs with the older couple. Susannah headed to them and sank to her knees on the sand. She filled them in on Shorty, then checked that they were all ok.

'Well done on the swim in, Carla. And you, Mel, great work on your own.' She turned to the other two, 'We don't know your names,' she said.

They introduced themselves as Mervyn and Sharon Welch and said they were glad Susannah seemed to be comfortable taking control.

'Well, I think we're safer here than on the boat,' she said. She glanced back down the beach. Silvio and Sam were supporting Shorty slowly towards them. As she watched, Silvio stumbled and almost fell. He and Sam sat Shorty down on the sand. She ran down through the sheets of cold driving rain.

'What's wrong?' she asked.

'I stood on something,' Silvio winced in pain.

Sam looked at Silvio's foot. 'Glass,' he said, 'Serious cut. Lucky you saved the first aid box, Susannah.'

Sam beckoned Mervyn, 'Give us a hand, mate?'

Finally, everyone was gathered under the meagre shelter of the wind torn bushes. Susannah turned her back on the rain. She cleaned and bandaged Silvio's foot as best she could. She used an alcohol wipe, and he sucked in his breath when it stung. She was sorry to hurt him, but she gently teased him as she worked. 'Now be a big brave boy. If you don't cry, you'll get a lolly pop when we're done.'

Sharon smiled and Carla laughed. Susannah was pleased to have been able to lighten the mood a little.

Suddenly Mel screamed. 'Oh God, look!' They followed her pointing finger, in time to see the boat crashing and splintering onto the black rocks.

'Well, that's that. Lucky we all got off. Now we must arrange a rescue,' Susannah said. She pulled out her phone and turned it on, relieved to see it wasn't wet. She wondered if there were enough tough plastic bags in the first aid box for them all to make a poncho for a bit of relief from the relentless driving rain.

Need at least one for Shorty, she thought.

CHAPTER EIGHTEEN

Ali Hadji's father drove into the entry of a large, harshly lit building. He carefully parked. In a grim group, they walked into the building. Despite the late hour, many people were moving purposefully about. Mr Hadji avoided everyone and led his sons towards the lifts.

On the fourth floor, the lighting was more subdued. At a long reception bench, three men were talking. One saw the Hadjis and came over to the group.

'Thank you for coming so promptly. I'm afraid this is a very difficult time for you. Please come this way,' he said.

He led them down a corridor and paused in front of a door.

'We have done everything we can. It is simply a matter of time.'

Ali squared his shoulders and followed his father and brothers into the dimly lit room.

On a high bed, he saw the slight form of his mother, a sheet pulled up to her chin. Her breathing was slow and shallow, rattling slightly. Her face was pale and serene, eyes closed, her dark hair tidily brushed out on the pillow.

The men bowed their heads and Ali's dad reached for his wife's hand.

One after the other, they said their quiet goodbyes, holding her hand or stroking her forehead. Ali was in turmoil. He was so glad to have made it home before she died but he was utterly saddened that his beautiful loving mother had been so cruelly taken by a stroke. He could not think further than this room and this moment.

His father's phone rang, and he stifled a gesture of impatience as he answered it with a brief word. Ali saw his father's stern face harden. 'He's here,' he said. He pushed the phone towards Ali and gestured him to leave the room.

Confused, Ali went into the corridor.

'Er, hello?'

'Ali Hadji?'

'Yes.'

'This is Mustafa Almasi. I am in Muswellbrook police station. They told me they needed an Arabic speaker. I have to ask some questions and translate for them.'

'The police?' Ali was stunned. 'No need for you,' he said. 'They can speak to me direct. I have good English.'

Ali listened in shocked silence to the policeman introduce himself and explain that he needed to know why Ali had left so suddenly.

'Look.' Ali tried to think how to say it briefly. He wanted to get back to his mother's bedside. 'I had a call that my mother had suffered a stroke and was not expected to recover. All I could think of was to get back here and be with her and my family. She is very near death right now.' He heard the waver in his voice.

'Oh gee, mate,' Ben said. 'I'm so very sorry to hear that and terribly sorry to have intruded just now. I'll give you and your family a few days and then I'm sorry, but I *will* have to get a bit more information from you. Your boss has been killed and we're questioning everyone.'

Ali fell back against the cold wall. 'Mr Hathaway?'

'No, *Mrs* Hathaway.'

Ali was appalled. He felt his heart breaking. He said softly, 'I don't think I can help you.' His brother put his head round the door and beckoned Ali. 'I have to go,' he said. He cut the connection and hurried back to his family.

In a very few moments, his mother quietly drew her last breath. At last Ali could let the tears slide silently down his face and was grateful for his brother's comforting hand on his shoulder.

Ben looked at the silent phone and then at Mustafa Almasi, his face troubled. *Poor Ali,* he thought. *I wish the silly bugger had explained to someone before he left, then I wouldn't have had to trouble him at such a tough time.*

'Well, Mustafa. Gotta thank you for coming in. Very helpful of you. Seems poor Ali Hadji's mum is dying and that's why he rushed off. Just sorry we seem to have wasted your time. But we'll pay you for the hour as we agreed. Was a lot easier than I thought and now we've got Mr Hadji's number, I should be able to get hold of Ali without your help. If I just say "Ali Hadji, please" Mr Hadji should understand, wouldn't you think?'

'Yer. Reckon Ali will get round to explaining why we rang so the father will be expecting it.' Mustafa stood up. 'Better get going now, got work.'

'Thanks again.'

Mustafa almost collided with Kaylee in the doorway as he left.

'I've got poison plants,' she said, jauntily waving the bag. Then she registered Ben's face. 'What's wrong?'

She listened as Ben explained. 'Oh dear, that's so sad. Poor guy. Oh well, we'll give him a few days and then go through the basic questions, but I'd fairly confidently say that rules him out, don't you think?'

Ben nodded soberly.

'Located your phone for you!' The techie swung casually through the door. Kaylee and Ben turned to him, grateful for the cheerful interruption.

'Place called Point Plomer, about an hour north of Port Macquarie.' He grinned smugly.

'Oh well done! Thank you!' Kaylee exclaimed, pulling out her phone. 'I'm going to give that girl such a snapping for wasting our time.' She quickly pressed the numbers.

'Hullo?' Susannah's mystified voice crackled indistinctly.

'Hello, Susannah. Its Detective Bradshaw here,' Kaylee kept her voice cool, relishing the success of locating the lovers without help from their families.

'Oh, Detective! Thank God! You're just who we need! The boat is smashed on the rocks and Shorty is terribly sick and Silvio has cut his foot. We're all freezing. You've got to help us,' Susannah gabbled.

'Whoa, whoa, Susannah! One thing at a time! Tell me slowly what's up,' Kaylee said. She heard Susannah gasp above the crackle of background noise. 'First of all, what is that noise? Are you in immediate danger?'

'No,' Susannah made a determined effort to get herself

under control even though she was shaking with relief.

'There's a huge storm. We went on a tourist cruise and the boat's engine broke down. A fuel line, I think. We've swum ashore but the boat is wrecked on the rocks.' Susannah couldn't help sobbing. Silvio put his arm round her shoulders.

'How many people? And how many injured or sick?'

Sam took Susannah's phone. 'Who is this?' After Kaylee identified herself, he took a breath of pure relief. He was so happy to know he was speaking to the police, it didn't occur to him to wonder why they wanted Susannah. He explained who he was and what had happened. He said he had activated the EPIRB but added he thought the weather too rough for them to be helped by sea. Kaylee put her phone on speaker and hissed at Ben to look up Point Plomer on his phone maps. Sam detailed Shorty's symptoms and said Silvio had a deep gash on his foot but that was bandaged and should be ok for now. He said they had no protection from the weather and added that two members of the group were elderly and showing signs of suffering from exposure. He said they had bottled water and finished up by stressing that he was very concerned about Shorty.

'Wait on,' Kaylee said.

She and Ben quickly located Point Plomer. 'Get on to Port Macquarie police, Ben. Tell them about the EPIRB. Say they need ambulances for Shorty and the two old people and transport for five others. Tell them roughly where to go.'

She turned back to the phone and spoke to Sam. 'Is your

phone working? Can you give Port Macquarie police an accurate location? Do you know the area? Is it accessible by road or only by sea?'

While he waited for Kaylee to come back on the phone, Sam had pulled his own phone from its zippered pocket and turned it on. He was thankful for the waterproof pockets on the life vests.

'I think I should call the police station at Port rather than triple zero,' he said. 'Could be quicker to organise a rescue. Can you give me their number? There's a road along the coast but it is unsealed and will be nearly impassable in this downpour. There'll be flooding to cope with as well.'

'You ring the police. They should be able to locate you using the emergency beacon or triangulation. Here's the number.' Kaylee rattled it off and then said, 'Now let me speak to Susannah.'

'Hullo?' Susannah sounded tentative.

'Susannah! Seems to me you've been having a bit of a hard time.' Kaylee's kind nature made her treat Susannah gently. 'But it sounds as if you have things well under control. We're organising things with the Port Macquarie police and we'll keep you updated with how the rescue is progressing. I need you to give me the numbers of all the phones that are working. It is important that you all conserve your batteries as much as possible so we can stay in touch. We don't know how long it will take to get to you. One phone to be turned on for five minutes every half hour. You understand we may not get you rescued tonight. Does your dad know where you are? Do you want me to call him and what about Silvio's parents?'

Susannah's voice came dejectedly through, 'Thank you. You're being very kind, and I *know* we made your job harder by going away. I'm very sorry. Dad and Burt don't know where we are, but I think if they find out about this disaster, Silvio's mum will have a fit. We're reasonably safe, just cold and hungry. So, please don't tell Burt and Dad. I think we'll be ok. I'm not sure about Shorty. He's just groaning in agony even though he's had pain meds ...' She trailed off uncertainly.

'Don't worry, Susannah,' Kaylee assured her robustly. 'We'll try to get things happening quickly. Have you got anything to keep Shorty and the two old people warm? How about you take someone with you and see if anything useful has washed up off the boat. Now give me those numbers and save your battery. Chin up, girl.'

When she finished talking to the detective, Susannah clicked the phone off. She turned to Silvio, seeking comfort from a hug. She quickly explained all that the detective had said. She noticed Carla's eyes widen as it dawned on her Susannah and Silvio were wanted by the police.

'Mel, will you and Carla come with me along the beach to see if anything has washed up that we could use for shelter?'

They left Sam talking to Port Macquarie police and struggled away towards the boat. They slipped and staggered in the sand squinting through the rain and the evening gloom, pushing against the wind.

'Hey, Boss,' came a voice as Kaylee hung up the phone after her conversation with Susannah.

'You'd better have more good news,' she grinned at

him. 'Things are starting to look up now that we've found Susannah and Silvio. Of course, no thanks to Mr Hathaway or Silvio's dad. They might be due for a severe little lecture about obstruction of justice or impeding a police investigation. But then again, they had no idea where their kids were. So, what have you got?'

'We've matched the fingerprint on the pot plant.'

'Oh, great! Who?'

'Darren Hathaway.'

'What!' Kaylee was incredulous. She stuck her head into Ben's office. 'Hey Ben, you've got to hear this.'

'That weak little nerd found the nerve to hit me over the head?' Ben exclaimed. 'Why ever would he do that?'

'We'll go first thing tomorrow and find out. I don't fancy another drive out there today, especially in this weather,' she replied, glancing out the window at the rain and the wind-tossed trees. 'I'll just get these plants to Clicks and then fancy a beer? I think we have finally made enough progress to have a little celebration.'

CHAPTER NINETEEN

I n the grey morning light at Point Plomer, the wind had eased but the rain still fell in sheets. Last evening, the foraging party had found a quantity of large plastic bags and two bench seats off the boat. They had managed to rig a rudimentary shelter by wedging the two seats at the base of the straggling bushes. They wrapped Shorty and Mervyn and Sharon Welch in the plastic ponchos they'd found in the first aid box to try to maintain their body heat. Under the meagre protection of the shrubs and a short protective wall of boat seats, they had all huddled together for warmth. They stretched the plastic sheets above themselves in a shaky, low roof that barely kept the rain off them. *I guess it is better than nothing,* Susannah mused.

She hadn't slept much, hadn't expected to. Her stomach was rumbling with hunger and her mind swirled in an agony of worry every time Shorty groaned. The night had seemed endless. She tried to use the time by clearing her mind, sorting through the mass of conflicting thoughts. Her mother's unsolved murder had started this whole rollercoaster of events. She had been comfortably enjoying her secret relationship with Silvio, working in a job she loved, enjoying living on the farm where she grew up. Life had been carefree and easy, even with the day-to-day difficulties of dealing with her mum. Now she felt responsible for a group of people she hardly knew, isolated in this dangerous storm. She acknowledged the nagging doubts that she had done wrong taking off to the coast with Silvio. *The police are not going to make life easy for me when I get back, and I deserve that.* She was so glad Silvio was with her and that he had willingly shouldered his share of responsibilities on this disastrous boat trip. She recognised that they had unconsciously worked naturally together helping get everyone off the boat, not questioning each other's judgement or decisions. *That is a good sign for our future together,* she thought.

She was relieved when she noticed the sky was finally lighting in the east. She was comforted to note that at last there were occasional breaks in the rain. She peered at the others and realised with a shock that Carla and Mel appeared to be sleeping soundly. She wasn't sure about the others and kept as still as possible to avoid disturbing them. Everyone looked very bedraggled, and she gave a passing thought to what a fright she must look. Then she shrugged ruefully, thinking that a good hot breakfast was probably more important right now than how she looked.

Suddenly she remembered they were supposed to turn on a phone on every half hour and quickly switched hers on. The battery level was beginning to drop, and she hoped the phone wouldn't die. She jumped when it started ringing.

'This is Sergeant Maddison from Port Macquarie police. Who am I speaking to?'

'Susannah Hathaway.' Relief made her voice shaky.

The sergeant asked for a quick recap on the situation. After listening to Susannah, he said they had two long-wheel-base rescue vehicles and a four-wheel drive ambulance on the road between Port Macquarie and Crescent Head, trying to locate the stranded group.

'Are there a couple of able-bodied people who could make their way inland to try to get to the road?' he queried. 'For safety's sake we need you to travel in twos and take an operating telephone with you. We'll move slowly along the road sounding the horn. As soon as you hear it, phone me. I'll text my number. Who will we be looking for?'

Susannah thought quickly. Much as she didn't want to be separated from Silvio, she figured it made sense for Sam and Silvio to try to make it through the low scrub towards the road. She told the sergeant who to expect and ended the call.

A quick chat with Silvio reassured her his gashed foot wasn't causing him much bother and wouldn't slow him down. Sam agreed she'd made the right decision, saying he and Silvio would be able to move pretty quickly across country. Sam switched on his phone and checked the battery level. Satisfied that it had enough power, he and Silvio set off.

Silvio turned and waved as they crested the dune.

'Good luck!' Susannah waved.

Then she turned her attention to the rest of the group. Mervyn and Sharon were sitting listlessly together, obviously cold but otherwise apparently all right. Mel was having a drink of water and Carla was stretching the kinks out of her legs. Shorty was mumbling and restless, either sleeping or unconscious. Susannah hoped it wouldn't be long before someone with the appropriate training could take over his care. She felt so helpless.

'Susannah?' Carla's voice was soft and shy.

'Mmm?' Susannah responded vaguely.

'Are you wanted by the police?'

Susannah jumped as if stung.

'Carla!' Mel's voice had the age-old tone used by mothers all over the world.

Mervyn and Sharon sharpened to attention, their eyes swivelling to Susannah.

'Well, we need to know, Mum,' whined Carla. 'What if she's a dangerous criminal?'

Susannah felt her face flaming. Her thoughts raced. She looked round the silent faces fixed intently on hers.

'Um, Susannah. Perhaps you should explain why the police got in touch with you specifically, when they had no way of knowing we needed their help,' Mel inched closer to Carla and put a protective arm round her shoulder.

Susannah squared her shoulders. 'The police were looking for me to help with a case they are working on. The only thing I have done wrong was not criminal, it was just a silly impulsive action.'

'I *knew* you weren't a bad person!' Carla's relief made her voice loud. 'Why would you be so nice and help us if you were bad?'

'No, I'm not a bad person,' Susannah said. 'But I have been a very selfish and thoughtless person. And I can't wait to get back and make up for it.'

'What did you do?'

'Carla! You're incorrigible,' Mel said.

'You have a right to know,' Susannah took time to get her response right for an impressionable teenager. 'I had a responsibility, and I ran away from it. I could have been helping the police but instead of that, they have been wasting their time looking for me.' She paused, then added, 'But in a way, it was a good thing they were looking for me. It has helped get our rescue underway. And the sooner we're all safe and dry, the happier we'll all be. I could really murder a burger with the lot and a heap of chips!'

She looked at their heads nodding eagerly and their faces relaxing. 'I think I've done some growing up, in these last few hours,' she added thoughtfully.

In the Hunter Valley, it was still showery and blustery.

Ben picked Kaylee up and they drove out to Divine Hayfields.

'Look at the branches and leaves all over the road,' Kaylee said 'If it was so bad here, miles inland, imagine what it must have been like for Susannah and Silvio on the coast without any shelter. I wonder how they got on. There was no news this morning so they must still be on the beach. This will be a test of character for both of them. I thought Silvio was a bit of a spoilt brat but maybe he has more backbone than I thought. Susannah seemed to be pretty much in control and up to the challenge.'

Life on the horse stud seemed to be calmly carrying on. The detectives could see activity around the big horse barn, but they carried on to the house, assuming Darren would not be involved in any of the manual labour.

Kaylee knocked on the open front door and raised her voice. 'Darren? It's the police.'

Once again, he wafted into the kitchen in his bright-patterned robe, hooking his glasses over his ears. 'What now?'

Kaylee thought he might be in for a bit of a shock, so she offered to make tea, casually asking where Mr Hathaway was.

'I guess he'd be down at the stables. Do you need him?'

'Well, no, Darren. We need you,' Kaylee made her voice firm and looked directly at him.

Beside him, Darren suddenly heard Ben's sharp voice. 'Why did you clobber me with that pot plant?'

Darren jumped. His face paled and he took an involuntary step backwards. 'W-w-what?'

'I asked, why did you clobber me with that pot plant?' Ben spoke slowly, emphasising each word. Darren's knees turned to jelly and he sat down suddenly on a kitchen stool. His shoulders drooped and he sank his head into his hands.

'Oh God, I'm sorry.'

'Here, have some tea and pull yourself together,' Kaylee said, pushing the cup towards him. 'Just start at the start and tell us your tale.'

Her calm words seemed to settle him. Darren straightened his back and took a moment to gaze out the window. Kaylee and Ben waited in silence, both deciding that in a few moments, Darren would open up. They were right. All the pent-up emotions and stress of his mother's death, his homosexuality (despite his bravado) and keeping his relationship with Kevin a secret, Susannah's absence, and his father's remote attitude made the words pour out of him.

'It's all too much! They can't accept that I'm gay. Dad just can't stand it, won't talk about it. I think Mum was coming round but now she's gone, and we don't know who killed her. I hate that. Zanna's wrapped up in Silvio and gone off somewhere with him. I miss her because at least she would talk to me. Dad is just burying himself in work and ignoring everything else. He's like a bear with a sore head. Mad at everyone and everything since Mum died. I know everyone thinks I just live for computers and that nerdy stuff, but I'm human, too. I have feelings, needs. I'm grieving for my mum. I get lonely. I want to be in a relationship, have someone who cares for me, someone I can care for, talk to, do things with. I found that with Kevin. We got together. He's sweet and vulnerable and kind and funny and we just talk and talk for hours. He's been so supportive for me just now. I don't know what will happen but he's all I've got, and I couldn't stand it if something happened to him ... if he went away ...' Darren trailed off.

Ben's mind was racing, processing the implications of Darren's relationship with Kevin. *Yet another complication,* he thought resignedly.

Darren gulped and continued, 'When I saw you follow Kevin that night, I just wanted to protect him. I didn't know what he'd done, why you were focusing on him. I just wanted to protect him.'

'Pretty extreme form of protection.'

Darren's face reddened uncomfortably. 'I know. It was

all I could think of. I'm really sorry. I'm no good at any of this.'

'So let me get this straight,' Ben said. 'You don't know if Kevin had anything to do with your mother's murder, but you decided to protect him anyway. What if he is her killer?'

Darren gasped. 'He can't be. No, he can't be!'

'Why not? Were you with him that evening? Have you two talked about it?'

'He texted me. He asked me what I'd done. If *he* did it, he wouldn't need to ask *me* what I'd done.'

'Sounds reasonable. Why do you think he asked you what you'd done?'

'I was upset that evening. He didn't go for a walk by himself. I was with him. I just needed someone to talk to, someone to hold me, someone to share the load. It can get pretty lonely in my family. He's so comforting and he knows how to make me laugh. I was fed up. Things are ... *were* always tense when Dad was away. You'd have thought Mum would be happy to run the place without him and without fighting about everything she wanted to do. But she'd just been on edge all day, changing her mind about everything every two seconds. None of us knew where we were. It was hell.'

'So, *had* you done anything?'

'NO! I didn't do *anything!* Mum and Zanna were stepping on glass with each other at dinner and I'd just had enough. I went to my room and texted Kevin about a walk.'

'Why were your mum and Susannah at odds?'

'Mum knew Zanna was seeing someone and Zanna wouldn't tell her who it was. Mum is ... was such a control freak, she always wanted to know everything. Dad always made her back off Zanna when she was at her, but he wasn't there. I made sure I kept Kevin and me a total secret. I can't imagine how she'd have reacted to THAT! But you know, when you're happy, you want to shout about it, and I couldn't do that. Everything all bottles up inside! She was nagging Zanna about who the guy was. Now I know why she wouldn't tell her. Mum would have gone ballistic if she knew it was Silvio. She thinks Burt is pretty much a low-life. But really, he's ok, straight talker, just a bit rough. Silvio is ok. Gisella is a bit of a volcano but she's kind-hearted.'

'We're not much further ahead,' Ben said. 'You hit me on the head to protect Kevin, but you don't know if he has done anything to need your protection. You claim you didn't have anything to do with your mother's death and you don't *think* Kevin did either but you're not sure because you were only with him while you were walking. You should be charged with assaulting a police officer and withholding evidence.'

'No!' Poor Darren looked to be on the verge of collapse.

Kaylee took pity on him. 'It's up to Ben whether he presses charges. What you did was pretty silly and could have seriously injured Ben. I fail to understand why everyone is lying about everything. I would have thought at least her family members would have wanted to quickly find your mother's killer. But you all seem to have secret lives that you are keeping from each other.'

'What happens now?' Darren quavered. He looked thoroughly crushed.

'What happens now is you and Kevin tell us absolutely everything you know. We frankly don't care about your relationship. We are trying to find a killer. And by the way, we've located Susannah. Once again it was done through police diligence, not by any help from you lot.'

Darren looked up, a hopeful expression partly erasing the lines of misery on his face. 'I swear I had no idea where she went, didn't know she was going anywhere until Dad asked me where she was.'

'Yes, well,' Kaylee continued sternly, not wanting to give him a break. 'It appears Susannah and Silvio simply decided the easiest thing to do was to take themselves off for a break at the coast. Quite thoughtless if you ask me. Fancy leaving a grieving family without letting anybody know their plans.'

'Actually, I can understand it,' Darren mused. 'Dad would have put his foot down and Gisella would have been hysterical. Yeah, I can totally understand them not saying anything to the parents, but they could have told *me*.'

'You apparently couldn't confide in your sister about *your* relationship. Why would she confide in you?'

Darren blushed again and nodded, recognising the point.

'So, Darren, is there anything at all you can tell us that might help us find your mother's killer?'

'I really can't. As I said, she made everyone defensive with her demands. What about Ali Hadji? He's disappeared. Did you check up on him?'

'Yes. Sadly, for Mr Hadji, he had to go home to Syria due to a family emergency. A pity he didn't think to let anyone know where or why he left, but it's pretty clear he had nothing to do with your mother's death. We still have to do the routine questions with him but we're giving him a few days to sort out his family stuff. Anyone else spring to mind? I seem to remember you were very nervous when we suggested that possibly Mr Bunrack killed your mum. Why was that? Do you know something about Mr Bunrack that might help us?'

Darren's face reddened again, and he looked guiltily around.

Here we go again, Kaylee groaned to herself. Why can't these people simply tell the truth?

'What, Darren?' she prodded.

'Umm, it's really nothing.'

'Can you let us decide that, please?' Ben spoke with remarkable restraint, carefully hiding his frustration.

'I was in town one day and I saw Burt talking to Yanko. He's a drifter, bit of a hippy, comes and goes. I caught a few words as I walked past, and Yanko was talking about harvesting the Kush. That's slang for marijuana, you know. I thought if Burt was involved in dope, I didn't want you guys sniffing round him. I mean, dope is pretty harmless, and I like Burt. I didn't want him to get in trouble through anything I said,' Darren said diffidently.

'Well, you've said it now,' Ben said. He carefully concealed his smugness about correctly guessing Burt's secret crop. He made a show of sighing with resignation. 'I guess we'll have to go and look into *that* as well. As if we haven't enough on our plate as it is. Pity the citizens of the Wheeler district weren't a little more law-abiding.'

'We might have a word with Kevin before we leave,' Kaylee suggested, trying hard not to smile at Ben's dramatics.

Darren stiffened and looked imploringly at Kaylee.

'We *must* do it, must thoroughly investigate everyone. This *is* a murder, you know!'

Kaylee turned and headed out the door, trying to hide her irritation. These people, she fumed in her head, can't seem able to stop themselves from lying and covering up.

'Come on, Ben. We'll probably find Kevin at the stables.'

She reached the front door on her way out and almost collided with Gordon striding up the steps. He looked thunderous, barely acknowledging the police officers.

'Hello, Gordon. You're in a hurry. Everything ok?'

'If you do not need to speak to me, I'm going to my office,' he muttered and brushed past them.

Gordon stormed inside. He had reached the end of his patience. His daughter was missing, damn her for not letting him know what she was up to. He was running a horse stud for *nothing* since his discovery that he was not to share in the inheritance, other than a miserable bloody pittance of a once-off bequest. Without Susannah, Ali Hadji and Hamish, everyone was working harder to stick to the program of preparing horses for the sale. He couldn't stand being in the same space as that bastard Mac. He was sick of the police seeming to be at the stud every moment. He was fed up with looking over his shoulder. Absolutely nothing was going to plan. He wanted to get back to Perth, back to Antonia. He missed her, and now it was doubly important for him to really forge a strong relationship with her. It wasn't going to develop the way he wanted it to if he stayed away too much longer. *How long will it be before the police will agree to me going back to Perth?* he wondered. He suddenly decided to leave. To heck with the fallout with the police and everyone. There was nothing for him here. He reached for the phone.

CHAPTER TWENTY

Ben and Kaylee walked quickly down to the barn. Kaylee wondered aloud if they should have told Darren not to text or phone Kevin.

Ben shrugged, 'Too late now.'

'Oh!' Kaylee stopped suddenly.

'What have you thought of?'

'Gordon was so obviously furious about something I clean forgot to tell him we had located Susannah and Silvio as well as Ali Hadji,' she said guiltily.

'I wouldn't worry about it. We only have an informal obligation to keep him abreast of developments. He hasn't been exactly forthcoming with us,' Ben said.

'But he must be worried about Susannah, she's his daughter remember.'

'He doesn't seem to be very worried about *anyone*, if you ask me. He's treating all this more as an inconvenience than a bereavement.' Ben shrugged. 'Or maybe he just does the stiff upper lip thing very well.'

They found Kevin working the mare in the lunging yard and took time to watch the beautiful animal going easily through her paces. Kevin scowled when he saw the police at the fence. He reined in the mare and walked over, hitching the rope to a ring on the fence.

'Have you spoken to Darren in the last ten minutes?' Ben decided to get straight to the point.

'No, why?'

'We've worked out that it was Darren who bashed Ben with the plant pot at the church the other night.'

Kevin stiffened. What has Dar told the cops?

'D'you have any idea why he would have done that? And please, do us a favour and be the first person in this investigation to tell us the truth straight up.'

Kevin's mind raced.

Ben pounced on the slight pause. 'All the lying is becoming tiresome,' his voice was harsh. 'Darren told us he saw me follow you and he decided you needed protecting so he bashed me. Why would you need protecting?'

'He thought I had something to do with his mother's death.'

'Did you?'

Kevin hesitated and looked away towards the mountains. An eagle was idly riding the thermals and Kevin wished he was up there too, literally "free as a bird".

'Oh please! Spare us the lies!' Kaylee burst out angrily.

'Ok! *Yes!*' He shouted. 'But I didn't kill her!' It was half a groan and half a wail.

Stunned, Kaylee and Ben looked at each other, eyebrows raised. Their shock would have been comical if the situation wasn't so grim.

'We would like you to talk us through your part in the events that took place here the night Mrs Hathaway died,' Ben spoke matter-of-factly, using the more formal phrases to give extra weight to his words.

Kevin sighed. Hesitantly, he started talking, his eyes still fixed on the soaring eagle.

'I guess Darren told you we're together. If not for him, I reckon I'd be gone by now. The day she died had been a day and a half. Day from hell, really. Mrs Hathaway couldn't make up her mind about anything. She changed her mind so many times that day. Kept contradicting herself, couldn't seem to settle on a firm plan. We were all fed up. After dinner, Dar texted, said he wanted to see me. He'd had a rough day too. Everyone was on edge. He was upset that his mum and his sister were at each other's throat. We walked and talked, just like any other couple at the end of a bad day. It was good just to have someone to unload on and we both felt better before we went our separate ways. Before I went back to my place, I wanted to check on the horses. I often do that last thing at night. To me it's very soothing to absorb the peaceful energy of the stable. Horses don't question you, they just accept you.' He sadly remembered that his parents had never "just accepted" him. He reflected that up to now he had done pretty well at managing his life without them and their repression. If only he could have avoided this horrible mess.

He turned to the mare and slowly stroked her satiny neck a few times. 'I use a little torch, so I don't disturb the horses. I walked into the barn, and I saw something about halfway along. I thought someone had left a chaff bag there and I was going to pick it up. I tell you, I got a bloody shock when I saw it was Mrs Hathaway.'

He went on stroking the mare's neck, eyes still on the graceful distant bird. 'I watched her but there was no sign of breathing. She was absolutely still, eyes open. Just sprawled on her stomach, head to the side. I couldn't help it ... all the rage and frustration boiled up in me. She was making everyone miserable, and she couldn't see it. I was sure she was dead ... I was relieved and angry and sorry for Dar and scared all at once. I wasn't thinking clearly. I suddenly realised I had the pitchfork in my hand, so I just shoved it into her. I don't remember getting it. I wished she could have suffered like we all did. I was appalled when I realised what I'd done. I wiped the fork handle with the sleeve of my sweater and ran out of the barn.'

'Is that the truth this time?'

'Yes! That's all I did. I watched her for a few minutes when I first realised it was her. My thoughts were swirling. I didn't see her chest or any part of her move. I swear she was dead before I ...' Kevin seemed to finally realise the enormity of what he'd done. He gasped. 'Her eyes were open. I swear she was already dead,' he added in a faltering voice.

'Does Darren know what you did?'

'No! Christ, how could I tell him I'd done that to his mother?'

'He'll have to know, I'm afraid. We can't just pretend it didn't happen. Kevin, you'll be charged with interfering with a corpse.'

Kevin's shoulders sagged. His arm was resting along the top rail of the lunging yard and he sank his head onto it. The mare seemed to sense his distress and gently rubbed her nose up and down his back. Kaylee felt sorry for him, but she knew there were procedures to be followed.

'You'll have to come back to the station with us.'

'Come on, we'll help you put the mare away,' Ben said.

'She'll need a rub down,' Kevin mumbled. 'Oh God! What will happen?'

'Calm down, mate. The court will be unimpressed that you didn't speak up straight away. But if you're telling the truth and if you have no prior convictions, you might be lucky to get a suspended sentence. Worst-case scenario, the maximum sentence is two years.'

Kevin staggered, his face ashen. Without seeming to realise what he was doing, he unhitched the mare and led her out of the yard to join Ben and Kaylee.

Ben walked thoughtfully beside him for a few steps. Then, appearing to come to a decision, he spoke.

'Look, Kevin. I've been thinking. We have one or two other things we need to follow up. Can we trust you to go to the station and hand yourself in? I'd suggest you get a solicitor to take with you. I want your vehicle make and rego. I'll phone all the information through to the police station. I'll tell them to issue an alert for your *immediate arrest* if you don't turn up or they don't hear from your legal representative within, say, ninety minutes.'

He turned to Kaylee. 'Ninety minutes should be long enough for him to get organised and get to town, don't you think?'

She nodded. 'Hurry up and clean yourself up. When you get to town, go to Legal Aid in Jaygar Street. Ask for Bevan Thornton. He's good and he should be available to help. He'll probably be able to get you bailed. If he can't get you to the station before your ninety minutes is up, ask him to phone the desk sergeant. Otherwise, there *will* be a warrant out for your arrest. But you just remember this, Kevin,' she said very sternly, 'if you run, if you let us down for trusting you, if you mess us up in *any* way, we'll make things turn out in the worst possible way for you. We're cutting you an enormous lot of slack out of the goodness of our hearts, and you probably don't deserve it after all the time wasted with lies and half-truths. Do yourself and us a favour and do what we've asked.' As she spoke the forceful words, she stood squarely in front of Kevin, making him meet her eyes.

'I will,' he mumbled, nodding. 'I feel a whole lot better now you know. Its bloody hard keeping secrets. I'll do anything to keep the fallout to a minimum, try and fix this mess. I've got to be able to keep working with horses. God! I've got to do everything I can to stay out of prison! Thanks for giving me a chance. Really, I won't let you down.'

He absent-mindedly held out the leading rope to Ben and hurried away, pulling out his phone, texting rapidly.

Meet me at the cottage. Hurry.

Ben looked at Kaylee ruefully. 'I hope we've done the right thing.'

'I hope *you've* done the right thing, you mean. What happened to consultation?'

'Ah, sorry. Spur of the moment, knowledge of country ways and all that,' Ben had the grace to look somewhat embarrassed.

'I guess you know best in that area. I think Kevin realises just how much he stands to lose if he jerks us around now.' She gave a short laugh. 'Looks like you've been left holding the mare. Let's find Jarred and hand her over. Then we can pay a little visit to the Bunracks.'

Ben gave a little crow of victory. 'Who's a clever boy picking Burt's little cash crop?'

'Ok, ok, clever you.' She patted his back mockingly. Then added, 'Do you think we should set their minds at rest about Silvio and Susannah?'

'Huh! If they show the least sign of carrying on with the lies and general unhelpfulness, they can go on worrying about Silvio for all I care.'

'I agree,' she nodded, and then pointed, 'There's Jarred over there.'

They changed direction to intercept him. His already frowning face grew heavier as they explained about Kevin.

'We're already running on skeleton staff. Mrs Hathaway gone. Hamish, Ali and Susannah all gone. Hell, I hope Kevin gets bail. Mac and I will have to rethink the whole program. We just can't handle the number of horses and get them in order for the sales without more hands. Gordon was going to see about putting on another lad, but I guess that slipped his mind. It's just me and Mac and Taj and Jason now. Gordon is in a black fury, not committing in any way to the decision-making, worse than useless.' Jarred looked guiltily over his shoulder as if expecting Gordon to be listening to his disrespect. His eye was caught by a running figure. Darren was heading towards the workers' cottage in a hurry.

Kevin heard the screen door crash open and called, 'I'm in my room.'

Darren dashed into the room and flung himself into

Kevin's arms. 'I'm sorry. I'm sorry. I'm sorry,' he mumbled over and over. 'They made me tell them about us.'

'Shh. Shh. Don't worry,' he murmured, stroking Darren's thin back. 'I need to know if you're with me. Will you stand by me no matter what?'

'Of course, always.'

'Think about it. This isn't a childish promise. I really mean it. Through thick and thin,' Kevin spoke harshly.

Darren leant back and looked, wide-eyed, into Kevin's anguished face.

He took a small step backwards and squared his shoulders, looking directly into Kevin's eyes. 'I'm here for you forever and always, no matter what,' he said though the hands that gripped Kevin's shoulders were shaking.

'I love you,' Kevin whispered. 'This means so much to me. Come on. I'll explain in the car.'

Kevin grabbed his wallet, took Darren's hand in his and ran out to his car.

As Kevin's vehicle sped off, Jarred sighed in frustration and went in search of Mac.

'What's the legal situation on this place since Mrs Hathaway's death?' he asked bluntly. He knew that the will instructed dispersal in favour of Mac, not Mr Hathaway, but he didn't know the details.

'Did you know Felicity was my mother?' Mac decided he'd better get people used to the truth if he was going to run the stud.

'You're kidding, right?'

Mac quickly explained the tale, watching Jarred's face. He was apprehensive about how his new status would be accepted.

'Wow! Who'd have thought it? So, you own this place now. You can do what you like.'

'Not really. Not yet. The solicitor said I'm to keep running the stud along the same lines as before and as a profitable concern until the will is finalised.'

'But you can make decisions, right?'

'What are you getting at?'

Jarred had been stressing about the situation on the farm and he didn't need further encouragement. 'We need more staff. If we can't get any extra hands, we're going to have to make some fairly drastic cuts to our list of animals for sale. I'm the manager and you're the owner. Stay here after we get through everything for today. Then what say we have a beer together and make some new plans.'

Jarred's enthusiasm spurred him on, despite Mac's cautious frown. 'We can present the ideas to Gordon as a done deal. His heart doesn't really seem to be in it. If we cut the list of animals to be sold because we're short-staffed, there will be too many horses here to be fed and cared for over the summer. So, we need to sell as close to the original numbers as possible. Have a think where we can source some workers while we finish up today's jobs. Then we'll have a beer and throw some ideas around. We don't have time to keep drifting on short-handed. What do you reckon?'

Mac realised this was Jarred's way of showing his support and acceptance. He also recognised the sense of Jarred's suggestions. He nodded, suddenly making up his mind.

'Right.' Then he frowned towards the road at a

fast-disappearing car. 'Where do you think Gordon's off to now?'

'Who knows? He hasn't exactly been sharing much lately. Forget about him. Think about the stud. I'll see you in the cottage round half-five.' Jarred shrugged off Gordon's departure. In his mind, he had already swapped Mac into Mr Hathaway's position as boss. He committed himself to supporting Mac in the absence of any meaningful recent support from Gordon. He already respected Mac and knew him to be intelligent and well informed on all things relating to running a horse stud. *We'll make a good team, Mac and I. Probably,* he thought, *Mac's only problem is his caution, but that will ease with experience.*

'Okay, I'll see you later.' Mac stepped away from Jarred. He phoned his wife to explain he wouldn't be home in time to look after their son after school. Then he phoned the local stock agent and asked him to locate at least two, maybe three temporary staff. When he finished that call, he had to take a moment to regroup. He had made his first independent decision about running the stud. Admittedly that was a very minor decision, but it was a step in the direction he intended to keep going. These days, he had trouble keeping his excitement under control at the thought that soon he would be doing this entirely for himself not just as a sort of caretaker. Ideas bubbled up, giving him extra energy to complete his tasks.

He mused as he continued working, not many guys get to inherit a long-established and successful horse stud. He was sorry if Susannah and Darren were unhappy with the way the will was left. He hadn't got a chance to discuss it with either of them. Gordon had made it absolutely clear he wanted nothing whatsoever to do with him now. He shrugged. *If Susannah and Darren want to continue working at Divine Hayfields, that is fine with me.* He knew Susannah to be a competent hard worker and he guessed Darren was keeping the books up-to-date. *I hope they will both be back soon. Why did Darren go with Kevin?* he wondered and fervently wished Kevin would get bail. *Right now, I need staff who are familiar with the way the farm runs. There isn't time to be training completely new staff.*

CHAPTER TWENTY-ONE

Once again, Ben and Kaylee drove in between the lion-topped pillars of Croham. This time, no noisy argument assaulted their ears as they approached the front door.

When Gisella opened the door, her eyes widened in fear, her hand flying to her mouth.

'Oh Dio!'

'Shh, relax, Mrs Bunrack. Please, Gisella, we're not here with bad news,' Kaylee said. 'Let us come in and talk to you. Is Burt here somewhere?'

Gisella gripped Kaylee's arm and led her through the house to the sunroom. Burt could be seen working the market garden on a small tractor.

'Sit down, Gisella,' Kaylee said. 'Just relax. Ben, can you get Burt in here?' Kaylee walked with Ben to the French doors and added under her breath, 'It would be too cruel not to set her mind at rest, poor woman.'

Ben nodded. He had forgotten how volatile Gisella was. No doubt she had been worried sick about her only child.

Burt hurried to Gisella's side. 'Well, what new 'assles have you brought us?' he demanded belligerently.

Kaylee looked at Gisella's strained face and said gently, 'We've located Silvio and Susannah. They're ok ...'

She got no further. Gisella burst into noisy sobs, rocking back and forth. Burt glared at the police and hugged his wife murmuring quiet words of comfort. Kaylee looked for a tissue box and handed it to Burt.

After a few minutes, Gisella calmed down. 'You sure they ok?' she demanded.

'Yes, they're fine. They were feeling stressed by all the trouble here and went to the coast for a holiday,' Ben's voice was casual.

'What?' Burt thundered. 'A bloody 'oliday? And we're all worried sick! I'll kill that boy so 'elp me, God!'

'You won't, you brute!' Gisella snapped.

'We're a bit cross with them too,' Kaylee said. 'The investigation into Mrs Hathaway's death may have moved along a bit more quickly if they hadn't taken off. They got stuck in that storm at Port Macquarie, so they won't be able to come home immediately. But,' behind her back, Kaylee crossed her fingers, 'they're fine.' She assumed the rescue operation was proceeding smoothly, making a mental note to call Port Macquarie police for an update when they left Croham.

She went on kindly, 'Gisella, you look like you could do with a strong coffee. Come into the kitchen and help me fix you one,' Kaylee said, giving Ben a meaningful glance as she ushered Gisella firmly out of the room.

Ben took her cue. 'Burt, we've found out you haven't been altogether truthful with us.'

Burt knit his brows. 'What now?' he growled.

'We thought it was a bit odd that you would have to grow potatoes secretly in a back paddock when you have the whole market garden to put them in.'

Burt looked up. 'Er, I told you. Just a little sideline,' he mumbled.

'It wouldn't be a little sideline of illegal marijuana, would it, Burt?'

'What? Shut up, can't you! Don't want Gisella knowing!' the farmer hissed. He stopped dead, realising he had let the cat out of the bag. 'Bugger! Bugger you, *and* yer damned questions!'

'Well now, Burt, tell me. Did Mrs Hathaway find out about your crop and threaten to dob you in, so you killed her? Is that how it happened?'

'*No!* For God's sake, no! Come outside! If Gisella 'ears this, I'm a dead man,' Burt implored.

Out of Gisella's hearing, Ben continued to question Burt. 'Are you quite sure, Burt? It seems a pretty good reason to kill someone: to shut them up?'

'Aw gee, you stupid cop, it wasn't like that! Felicity annoyed the 'ell out of me and 'alf the district, but she didn't know about my crop, and I didn't kill her.'

After some thought, Ben said 'So, what are we going to do about this little crop of yours if what you're saying is true? Because last I heard, growing marijuana was illegal just like murder is.' He paused to let Burt digest his words. Then added, 'The way I see it, Burt, you've been greedy.'

'Look, I never killed Felicity. I'm not a total idiot! But that crop, well, yer can't blame a chap when 'e's on a good thing,' Burt grumbled.

'Have a little think about it, Burt. Do you want Gisella to know? Do you want to have a full police investigation into this?'

Burt stood truculently shaking his head.

'Look, we only found out about this as an aside, really, during the murder investigation. I don't want to go through all the paperwork and carry on of prosecuting you. Up to now, as far as I can tell, in every other respect you are conducting a perfectly lawful business. You've had a couple good years extra income from the dope. But it's coming to a stop *right now*!' Ben's voice hardened. 'I'm going to have a word with your mate Yanko. I'll tell him you had an unfortunate fire in your back paddock. Then I'm going to suggest he move on and warn him about starting any more crops anywhere else. I strongly advise you to have a thorough burn of that paddock and I advise you to get it done very quickly, like this afternoon. Fire permits aren't mandatory this early in spring, so you have no excuse. I'll be checking in a couple of days and if you can't show me a burned off paddock, the first person to hear about it will be Gisella and the second people will be the police drug squad. And then we will dig and dig until we get some evidence pointing to you as Mrs Hathaway's murderer. Do I make myself clear, Burt?'

Burt threw up his hands in surrender. 'Yes! You've made your point. I'll 'ave a bloody fire up there! You're a rotten killjoy is all I can say.'

'Careful, Burt. I think I hold all the aces here, so you'd best watch your mouth. Do I have your word there will be a fire in the back paddock very, very soon? Don't double-cross me or you will be dealing with Gisella *and* the police.'

Burt finally gave in. He looked Ben in the eye and held out his hand. As Ben shook it, Burt said, 'Fair enough. You've given me a chance and I'll take it. Anyway, you'd never find evidence I killed Felicity because I didn't do it. Gisella's been hit 'ard by Felicity's death and Silvio running away. She don't need any more grief. I'll 'ave a fire. Just make sure you warn Yanko off properly, I don't want 'im turnin' up 'ere with a grievance.'

Burt realised he had been in danger of letting his lawless, reckless youth from Croydon resurface. He knew he couldn't jeopardise his farm, marriage and comfortable life with that foolishness. Secretly, he was relieved that the police were forcing him to make the decision to abandon the dope.

'Thanks, Burt. I'll deal with Yanko. Just stick to the straight and narrow from now on. You've got too much to lose.' He gestured at the orderly paddocks and the gardens. 'And there'll be no second chances, Burt. Make sure you understand that.' He paused, then turned towards the house, 'I'd say Kaylee's got Gisella settled with a coffee now. Come on back in.'

*   *   *

In the easing rain, Silvio and Sam stumbled through the rough undergrowth and sandy soil. Silvio's foot was painful, but he trusted that Zanna had cleaned it well and he knew she had wrapped it firmly. He was surprised at her practical skill and her calmness. He knew his mother would have been unable to treat an injury like that, she would have been hysterical. He grinned at the thought.

'What's to laugh about?' Sam asked. 'I thought you and your girlfriend were wanted by the police.'

Silvio snapped a glance at him. 'Well, not really wanted in the criminal sense, mate. We were helping them in an investigation, and it just got overwhelming. Susannah's recently lost her mother. We just decided to get away.'

'Oh, sorry.' Sam felt bad for letting his curiosity get the better of him.

'You weren't to know. To tell the truth, I've been feeling bad about us going away because we didn't tell anyone where we were going. They've all been worrying themselves sick and the police have been spending time looking for us instead of moving on with the investigation. We've been pretty irresponsible,'

Sam didn't want him dwelling on his dark thoughts. Privately, he was glad both Susannah and Silvio had been so level-headed and very willing to lend a hand. He knew things could well have ended far worse without having them to rely on. To brighten the mood, he repeated his question about Silvio laughing.

'Oh, that,' Silvio grinned again, 'I was just comparing Zanna dealing with my foot last night with how my mother would have dealt with it. She's very volatile, can be right up in a moment and then a complete mood change in seconds!' He frowned again, 'I wish we'd handled things better. Poor Mama. Wait!' He interrupted himself, 'Is that a horn?'

They stood still and listened. 'Yes!' Sam said, dragging

the phone from his inner pocket. He quickly rang the number the police had given Suzannah.

'We can hear the horn! We'll keep heading west and you keep blowing the horn.'

They quickened their pace as much as they were able in the soggy, clinging underbrush, both feeling cheered by the knowledge that rescue was close.

In a short time, they could see the vehicles and began waving and yelling.

It felt good to be able to hand control to people who were qualified to deal with their situation. The police said they'd seen a rough track heading towards the beach not far back along the road, so Sam and Silvio jumped in, and the little motorcade set off.

The two police four-wheel drives cautiously led the way along the washed-out sandy track. The ambulance crept carefully behind them. Sam and Silvio were in the leading police vehicle. They drove down onto the beach and Sam pointed to the north.

'There are the rocks the boat wrecked on. The others are up close to that.'

When they heard the engines of the approaching cars, Susannah, Carla and Mel stood up and started waving wildly. Relief made Susannah's knees weak, but she forced herself to stay calm and be helpful. Food in the form of bananas and nut bars was welcomed although it was a far cry from the burgers and chips Susannah and Carla had been longingly imagining.

The ambulance officers quickly assessed Mervyn and Sharon. 'Looks like nothing that a hot shower and a good night's sleep won't fix. You're both in good shape, but we'll get Emergency to give you a proper once over just to be safe.'

Shorty was carefully checked out. The decision was that he may be suffering appendicitis and should travel in the ambulance directly to hospital.

'Can you check out Silvio's foot as well?' Susannah felt unsure of her expertise and wanted to hear a professional opinion.

After a few minutes' activity, the police and ambulance officers reached a quick discussion.

'Here's what we'll do. Shorty will go to hospital in the ambulance. Mervyn, Sharon and Silvio will go with Officers Davis and Martin to hospital Emergency. That foot was well bandaged, Susannah, but needs stitching. I'll take Sam, Susannah, Mel and Carla back to the station and we can do the reports. Then I'll drop you at the waterfront and you can pick up your cars. It'll be a slow trip for us all because the road is a mess. There's localised flooding in town but now the rain's easing that should be subsiding. You guys picked a rough night for your adventure, but you all seem to have come through reasonably well. Well done. It looks like you kept your heads and cooperated. Without that, this could have ended very differently. Right, let's not delay.'

While Shorty was loaded gently into the ambulance, Silvio and Susannah took a minute together. He hugged her tight. He voiced the concerns he had spoken earlier to Sam and felt Susannah cling tighter.

'Yes, I know,' she said. 'I've been feeling very bad too,

Sil. But we're on our way back now. So, we can soon start making up for all the trouble we caused.'

'Hey, Silvio,' Sam called. 'Don't leave town without catching up. I'd like to thank you properly for all the help you and Susannah have been. I'd have been struggling without you.'

'For sure, mate. We'll see you later today.'

'Okay, everyone. We've got Shorty loaded. Let's not muck around. Don't want the tide running us out of beach and trapping us. In you get.'

The doors slammed and Susannah heaved a sigh of relief as they headed towards safety and a hot shower.

CHAPTER TWENTY-TWO

Gordon parked in the long-term carpark of Sydney airport. He grabbed his bag and briefcase, locked the car and strode into the airport building. After checking-in for his flight, he headed up to the VIP lounge to wait for take-off to Perth.

Looking every inch the successful businesswoman, Antonia sat comfortably at her desk. Her camel-coloured crepe dress fell softly, framing the amber necklace around her throat. She was engrossed in the report she was reading and reached absent-mindedly for her phone when it rang. She stiffened to attention when she saw it was Gordon calling.

Shifting gears mentally, she sweetened her voice. 'Gordon, how lovely to hear from you. How are things going?'

'Antonia, so good to hear your voice. How I've missed you! I couldn't stay away from you any longer. I'm booked on flight 88A, arriving about 4:30 pm your time.'

Antonia flinched. Damn! Her mind raced, I thought he'd be held up over there a bit longer.

'I should be able to pick you up,' she said calmly, 'Just let me check my diary.'

'I can't wait to see you. It's been just hell over here and the police are completely incompetent. Couldn't sort out who sneezed in a pepper factory, let alone solve a murder. I need some sanity and peace.'

'You'll be away from it all soon,' she said soothingly. 'My diary is clear. I'll pick you up. You can tell me all about it over dinner tonight ... we *will* be having dinner, won't we?' I'd better sound devoted, she thought, make him feel needed.

'Yes, of course! I want to see you as soon as possible. You're very good for me, a true tonic,' Gordon thought he should sound distressed at how long they'd been apart. *It's high stakes now that I make this relationship work, she's my meal ticket,* he thought callously. 'I've really missed being able to see you, talk to you,' he laid it on.

'It won't be much longer. I'll see you at the airport pick-up spot.'

She hoped she sounded sufficiently affectionate and concerned. She mentally cursed the timing and then called Logan.

'Hey, you,' Logan spoke cheerfully.

Without a greeting, Antonia spoke rapidly, 'Gordon just phoned from the airport in Sydney. He'll be here this afternoon. What's the situation?'

'Damn, that's a bit sudden. Have the police wrapped up their investigation into his wife's death?'

'I don't know. I was struggling to get myself into "loving partner" mode and didn't ask any questions. We're having dinner tonight and then I guess he'll want me to spend the night, so I'll have plenty of time to get some answers.'

'Well, there's probably no rush. I can't see him just

toddling over to see his lover for a couple of nights only to dash off again if things weren't under control back east. I'd say he'll be here at least a week, maybe more, so we've got time to get things set up. Just find out all you can. I'll set a few things in motion and give you a call later tomorrow. Don't worry. We hold all the aces, and we can act in our own time. Good thing he rang and let you know. You'd have found it even more of a challenge getting into "loving partner" mode face-to-face,' Logan chuckled.

'Shut up,' Antonia snapped. 'I like more time planning and preparing, I'm not the spontaneous type. I don't like surprises.'

'Chin up, girl,' Logan said heartlessly. 'You don't have to be an adoring lover for too much longer. And think of the easy money,' he added encouragingly.

'That's a fair point,' she conceded. 'I'll talk to you soon.'

She took a few minutes to regroup, concluding that the two pluses right now were that the end of her charade relationship was in sight and the financial reward was close to being a reality. *At least I've got all day to get into the right frame of mind,* she reasoned, getting back to work.

✳ ✳ ✳

Kaylee and Ben were in the police car, heading back into town.

'You WHAT?' Kaylee exploded. 'Ben, you can't just sweep a dope crop under the carpet!'

'Let's look at this as a continuation of your rural policing education,' Ben spoke reasonably. 'We need to do as much as possible to keep the community on our side. Farming is hard work with unreliable rewards. The way I see it, Burt was supplementing his income. It *could* have gone on indefinitely. But this way, Burt has had his little bit of extra income and it stops now. We have shut down the dope crop, there will be no income from it this year. Burt knows that we can be fair, but he can't pull the wool over our eyes. There'll be no ongoing resentment from him, especially if Gisella never finds out about the crop. I'll be warning off an undesirable from our area of responsibility. I'll send out a warning to all the other state stations about Yanko. He'll slip up soon and get caught. I know it's illegal to grow dope, but I've shut that down here, now. Anyone who knew about Burt's little venture will see that it is a poor idea and not worth trying. I will *definitely* check that Burt burns the paddock, and I will *definitely* give Yanko a strongly worded warning. I think you'll agree that we're busy enough right now without any extra paperwork. Most importantly, it has been a solid reminder to us that we need to be vigilant all the time about what's going on across the whole community.'

'Wow. Do all rural police commands work this way?'

'There is a large degree of give and take. The reason is that rural police commands are forever short-staffed. In many instances, if it wasn't for the goodwill and assistance of the community, rural policing would be almost impossible. Of course, you have to use judgement. What may work in one situation may not work in another. A good relationship is a very valuable asset but remember, it's a fine line between cutting a little slack and maintaining respect and cooperation.

Not to mention maintaining law and order in the accepted sense. The public needs to be sure we're looking out for the greatest good. You saw with the fundraiser, how they all pull together. They're proud of their community and happy to act independently for what's best for themselves. All they really want of the police is that they support local goals and keep things safe and above board.'

Kaylee looked out her side window while she processed Ben's carefully delivered lesson.

Her eyes widened in horror. She had time for a sharp indrawn breath before CRASH!

A truck laden with heavy farm equipment didn't pause or give way before turning onto the road. Ben had no time to do anything other than jam on the breaks. Their car was rammed across the road and spun into the trees.

Ben became aware of the car horn sounding continuously and irritably wished it would stop. Gradually as he regained his wits, he realised his arm was stuck between the airbag and the steering wheel, pressing on the horn. He sat up, struggling with the airbag, trying to collect his scattered wits. He could hear someone yelling but he couldn't process the words, much less figure out who was shouting. He heard a soft moan. Hell! Kaylee!

He shouted, 'Kaylee, are you ok? Can you hear me? Answer me, Kaylee!'

In mounting horror, he struggled with his seatbelt and the airbag. *Oh, God,* he thought, *focus. Remember your training, you fool.* Gradually his senses cleared. He undid the seatbelt at last and started struggling to open the door. It was jammed tight shut. He dragged away at the airbag and finally cleared it so he could see Kaylee. He realised slowly that she wasn't the person shouting. She was slumped in the seat, blood running from her head.

A second CRASH shocked him! What now? He groaned and tried to concentrate.

'Don't move! Don't move! You could have spinal injuries. Stay still. I've called the ambos and the police. Just stay still. I've smashed the back window. Reckon you'll have to come out that way.'

Ben groaned again and tried to assess his injuries. He felt bruised and battered and only about half alert, but he couldn't feel anything specifically causing him sharp pain. His head ached and his right arm hurt, but he couldn't see any blood on himself, and everything seemed to be moving as it should.

He yelled towards the back of the car, 'Get the first aid box out of the boot and grab something for Kaylee's head. She's bleeding a lot. Hurry up, pass it up to me.'

Scrabbling sounds in the back and then, 'Here.'

'Thanks.' Ben grabbed the dressing and carefully pressed it on Kaylee's forehead. While holding it firmly in place, he looked for other injuries, scared that her neck was broken. *How long, how long for the ambulance,* he thought desperately. *Was that a siren?* He held his breath and listened.

Kaylee moaned again. 'Shh, shh. Kaylee, stay still. We've been in a smash. Open your eyes if you can.'

While maintaining firm pressure on the bandage with his right hand, Ben groped around until he was holding Kaylee's hand in his left.

'Squeeze my hand if you can hear me, Kaylee. But don't

try to move anything else. Help is coming.' Did he feel a slight pressure from her fingers?

Suddenly, he was sure he could hear the siren approaching. Thank goodness!

'Not long now, Kaylee. Can you open your eyes or at least squeeze my fingers?'

'Bloody hell! You're a nag, Benny boy, did you know that? Can't you leave me in peace?' Kaylee's voice was weak, but her words were strong.

'Oh, so you're fine, then! Glad to hear it.' Relief made Ben's voice rough. 'Just stay still. Any pain?'

'Yes! You're pressing horribly on my forehead, and it really hurts to breathe. Are you ok?'

'Sorry. I have to keep pressure on your forehead, its split and bleeding. You must have hit it on the window. Maybe you've busted a few ribs too. Can you feel your legs and wiggle your toes?'

In the pause while she tried, he heard a couple of vehicles pull up. It was hard to know what was actually happening because their car had finished up facing away from the road.

'Is that you, Ben?' He heard the familiar voice of Sergeant Phelps. 'Give me a quick rundown on things if you can, mate.'

'Glad you got here so quick, Rob. A truck hit us on the passenger side. We spun out. Driver's door is jammed, and I guess so is the passenger door. I'm ok, bruised, dazed. Kaylee is bleeding from the forehead, and we think she's got broken ribs, says it hurts to breathe. Who was it gave me the dressing and broke the rear window?'

'Ahh, that was the guy who hit you. Bloody careless driving! Guess he feels terrible and was keen to help. Just from a quick look over things, I don't think either of your doors will open. I think once the ambos have given you the once over through the window and pass you fit, we'll try to get you out through the back window. Not sure about Kaylee. Depends on her injuries. I'm going to pass you in a plastic sheet. Spread it between Kaylee and her door to protect her and we'll smash her window, see what's what with her.'

'Did you get all that?' Ben asked Kaylee.

'Yes, mate,' she sighed wearily. 'It's my ribs that hurt, not my ears.'

Ben lowered his voice. 'Now just between you and me, can you remember what we were talking about before the crash?'

'Yes,' Kaylee sounded mystified.

'What I said about give and take in rural policing?'

'Yes.'

'Well, this guy is getting the book thrown at him. He should know *never* to assume country roads are free from traffic,' Ben said grimly.

'But hey, wait a minute,' she protested, 'what about "assistance of the community"? The driver *gave* assistance, rang our rescuers, got you bandages for my head. Is it one set of rules for Burt and another set for this guy?'

'You've got a point,' Ben said grudgingly. 'Glad you listened so carefully to the lesson. But we can't sweep this entirely under the rug.'

'No, I agree. But rather than throw the book at him, let's

get Rob to be sure to give him the minimum. I mean, he's just another farmer on an unreliable income like Burt and he stayed to help.'

Ben gave her a mock salute. 'You're the boss!'

'Hey, Ben. Grab this plastic sheet and spread it. We'll break the window so Kaylee can be given a basic assessment. Her door is mangled but looks like we might be able to lever it open with the truckie's crowbar.'

In a relatively short time, Ben and Kaylee were out of the wrecked police car. Against Ben's protest of being "absolutely fine", he and Kaylee were shepherded towards the ambulance.

'Rob, don't go too hard on the truckie, he gave us all the help he could,' Ben muttered.

'I understand, Ben, don't worry.' Rob slapped him on the shoulder. 'Now go and get patched up. We need you both back in the office as soon as possible.'

Ben looked back at the mangled police car. *Huh,* he thought, *so much for saving paperwork on Burt! Reporting on this is going to be a pain.*

CHAPTER TWENTY-THREE

Antonia was glad the airport pick-up zone forbade drivers from leaving their cars. This way she avoided a big welcoming hug, merely leaning over to give Gordon a peck on the cheek before pulling out into the traffic.

'Are we going to the Crowne Plaza?'

'Yes,' Gordon sighed as he stretched his legs, enjoying the comfort of her BMW. 'I booked my usual suite. Did you have any ideas for dinner?'

'Let's just use the restaurant in the motel, save going out again. I'm sure you're ready for a few quiet days after what you've been through,' Antonia hoped she sounded caring and considerate. 'I'm guessing the police have found your wife's murderer, since you're over here.'

'No!' Gordon replied shortly. 'I was just fed up with it all. I don't see why they need to keep me over there in this day and age of mobile phones.' Abruptly, he changed the topic. 'Can you stay the night?'

'Yes, of course. I've rescheduled a few things, cleared my calendar a bit. But there are some things I can't defer, I'm afraid.'

Mentally changing gears to sound more like the

returning lover and less like the grumpy traveller, Gordon said, 'That's fine. I've some business of my own that'll be taking up a bit of time. Just so long as we have tonight to relax together and catch up.'

Antonia's mind had been racing during the drive to the hotel and she thought she might have a workable plan evolving.

In the suite, while Gordon freshened up, she quickly texted Logan, *I'll suggest we go to the races on Saturday. Maybe things could happen there.*

The phone pinged a message almost immediately, *Great idea. I'll set things in motion.*

Both Antonia and Gordon felt the need for a relaxing drink before dinner. It was going to take them both a little while to get back into act of seeming devoted to each other. He was trying to be interesting and interested, she was trying to be consistently amenable and sympathetic. She was genuinely interested to hear the details of the investigation into Felicity's murder. It was intriguing to speculate who the killer was. She wondered how likely it was that the police would order Gordon to return to the farm. She was privately stunned at how quickly life on the stud had apparently unravelled and the mass departure of staff and family members. She thought Gordon seemed pretty blasé about his daughter's disappearance, more concerned with how her relationship with Silvio would affect his image. She was amused by his distaste for Darren's homosexuality. *Get yourself into the twenty-first century, Gordon,* she thought sardonically.

By the time they went downstairs to the restaurant, they

were both feeling more comfortable in their adopted roles.

'Other than your business commitments, did you have plans for while you're here?' Antonia tried for a neutral topic while they shared a plate of bruschetta as a starter.

Gordon looked up and met her eyes, his expression earnest. 'I'm afraid all I could think of was seeing you,' he said disarmingly. 'I know it was short notice for you and I understand that you can't just stop your work for me. I need to catch up on how things are going with my business over here and check in on my sister but other than that, no plans.'

'Well, how about I introduce you to horse racing Western Australian style?' Antonia smiled across the table.

Gordon's mind raced as he anticipated rubbing shoulders with people in his familiar setting. What a great opportunity to meet well-connected people and perhaps some of Antonia's friends, maybe even be introduced as her partner. Perfect way to get his foot in the door.

'I'd love that,' he responded with genuine enthusiasm.

'Wonderful. I'll book us a table in the Director's Lounge. I'm sure you'll be right at home,' Antonia said warmly.

* * *

As soon as the necessary reports were completed at the police station, Mel, Carla, Susannah and Sam were driven back to the dolphin cruise carpark. Susannah quickly swapped numbers with Mel and Sam.

'Mel, if you ever want a country holiday, call me. I live on a horse stud in the Hunter Valley.' Susannah smiled at

Carla's expression of excitement and knew she would see them at Divine Hayfields one day soon.

'Maybe we can catch up this evening,' she said to Sam. 'I'll call or message once I've picked up Silvio.' Sam nodded and gave her the thumbs up as she quickly climbed into her car, anxious to see Silvio as soon as possible.

She followed the signs across town to the hospital but had to make several detours because many roads were still cut with flood waters or impassable with debris. She was grateful that the reporting at the police station had been straightforward. She reminded herself to check in with Detective Bradshaw after she'd picked up Silvio.

Mervyn and Sharon had been discharged by the time Susannah reached the hospital. She found Silvio with his foot tidily bandaged, dozing in a cubicle.

'Hey, wake up! You don't get to sleep while I do all the work!' She threw herself onto the narrow bed and welcomed the warm circle of his arms around her.

'Ohh, can't wait to get back to our motel! Are you all finished here? Do you know what happened to Shorty?'

Silvio silenced her with a long kiss.

After a bit, he said, 'They told me Shorty has gone straight to theatre to have his appendix out. Apparently, he's a pretty sick lad. Mervyn and Sharon are fine, and I would guess they're probably tucked up sleeping like exhausted babies,' he smiled.

'Poor Shorty. I'm glad they got us rescued when they did, or he might be in even worse shape.'

'I agree. I'm all good to go. Have to get the stitches out in about a week, they said.'

'Great!' Susannah jumped up and grabbed his hand. 'Hot showers, food and bed for us! But we'll have to be awake again by this evening. Sam wants to catch up before we leave town.' She paused. 'I guess we'll be leaving town tomorrow?'

'Yeah, love. I think it's time we faced the music,' Silvio said soberly.

'Oh heck, I keep forgetting to ring Detective Bradshaw,' Susannah said guiltily.

'Do it now. Get it out of the way.'

Susannah tried Kaylee's number and it went to message bank. She tried Ben's number and after a long delay, Ben answered.

Suddenly, Susannah felt awkward and paused while she tried to think what to say. Finally, she managed, 'It's Susannah Hathaway,' in a quiet voice.

'Susannah! Are you and Silvio ok?' Ben sound oddly shaken and she couldn't think why.

'We're fine, thanks to you and Kaylee putting the rescue in motion ...' she paused, embarrassed. Then she rushed on, 'I just wanted to say how very sorry we are for all the fuss we caused. Is Kaylee, er Detective Bradshaw, with you? Can I talk to her?'

Ben took a moment, trying to find the softest way to break the news of their crash to Susannah. 'Well, Susannah, there's a bit of bad news up here ...'

'What's happened?' As usual, Zanna's practical nature helped her sound calm, although her heart was in her mouth.

'We went out your farm to talk to Kevin. And to let your

folks and Silvio's know you two were ok. But we were in a smash on the way back to the station.'

'Oh no! Are you ok?'

'We're still at the hospital. Have to wait for x-rays and so on. Looks like Kaylee has broken ribs. There's a gash on her forehead, too, that needs stitching.'

'I'm so sorry to hear that. We're at the hospital too. Sil had to have his foot stitched. One of the guys that was with us had emergency appendix surgery. The rest of us are ok, just tired. Oh dear, things are in a real mess, aren't they? Poor Kaylee and what a lot of extra worry for you. Look, Silvio and I realise we were both very selfish and stupid. We're anxious to get back and try to help in any way we can, as we should have all along, instead of running away to the coast.'

'It doesn't sound as if it was a very relaxing break away, after all.' Ben chuckled slightly. He thought Susannah sounded as if she had grown up overnight into a much more thoughtful and assured person.

'No,' Susannah agreed, relieved to hear Ben sound a bit more normal. 'Are you ok? You only mentioned Kaylee's injuries.'

'Yeah. Just a few bruises, I think and shaken up. When will you be back?'

'The roads are a mess of branches and mud. It's too late to drive safely up that mountain road today and besides neither of us had much sleep on the beach last night.'

'Ha! I can imagine. Must have been pretty awful.'

'It was. But we're fine. We'll get a good rest and head up

tomorrow. D'you think you'll be at the office, or should I call you?'

'Just give Kaylee or me a call when you hit town. She may be in hospital, not sure. But one or other of us will be able to speak to you. Travel safely.'

As he ended the call, Ben suddenly realised he hadn't phoned the station to alert them to look out for Kevin. *Oh heck,* he groaned, *I really hope he did the right thing and turned up. Guess I can fill in some of this wait time at the hospital by checking up on that.*

❋ ❋ ❋

Kevin had driven carefully into town. He didn't want to miss his ninety-minute deadline, but he wanted time to explain everything to Darren. Except for a few exclamations, Darren had listened to Kevin's confession without interruption. When he had finished, a heavy silence filled the car. Kevin was filled with alarm that Darren wouldn't be able to accept what he'd done. His thoughts ran away with all sorts of worst-case imaginings. He was having difficulty keeping his mind on driving and even more difficulty staying quiet while Darren processed all he'd said.

Finally, Darren spoke. 'Wow! I mean, wow. That's a hell of a lot to get my head around. Bloody hell!' He paused, then went on. 'Are you sure Mum was, was, um, already gone when you did that with the fork? Are you really sure?'

'Of course, Dar. I watched her for a while, and she never moved. Her eyes were open.' Kevin felt sick to be telling Darren the terrible details.

'And did you mean all you said about our relationship meaning so much to you?'

'Darren, you're my world,' Kevin said simply. 'You're supportive, funny, clever ...' he faltered to an uncertain stop. The truth was he relished everything about his relationship with Darren. It filled the hole that his unloving parents had made. In all his travels working on farms in eastern Australia, he had never met anyone who had given him such confidence, who made him believe he was someone worthwhile, who made him so happy and fulfilled.

'One of the cops said Mum might have been poisoned. Did you do that?'

'NO! How could I have done that? I wouldn't know how to! I've never even been in your house.' Kevin was appalled at the direction Darren's mind was travelling.

Darren turned his eyes sadly to Kevin. 'This is such a horrible bloody thing. I'm sorry but I had to ask you, I had to be sure. I really miss Mum but you've been so solid for me. I wish you hadn't, hadn't got involved. I wish you didn't have this police stuff hanging over you.' Darren sounded as confused as he felt, his thoughts jumping from one tack to another. 'We haven't really had a chance to enjoy ourselves together. We've always had to sneak around. But it hasn't all been just sharing our stresses, has it?'

'No, my hunky Dar,' Kevin said gently. Dared he hope Darren wasn't going to ditch him? 'No. We've had more than just stress. We've laughed together, shared our dreams with each other.'

'Kevin, I meant what I said, too. It's been really awful, and we probably got the world's worst start to a relationship, but you make me feel so strong. You make me feel like I can beat the world. We can get through this if we're together. Through thick and thin, like you said.' He reached across and rested his hand on Kevin's.

A brilliant smile lit Kevin's face. He thought relief might make him drive off the road. 'Oh, thank God!'

Darren squeezed Kevin's hand. 'Let's get this thing done. I'm right beside you every step. If they give you bail, I can pay if it's too much for your funds. Together, right?' he said firmly.

'Together,' Kevin agreed solemnly.

* * *

By late afternoon, after a sound sleep, Susannah and Silvio were refreshed and hungry again. Silvio rang Sam and arranged to meet him at one of the many pubs on the waterfront.

They settled down at a table and began to rehash their adventure over beer and burgers. They gave Sam an update on Shorty, adding he'd probably be in hospital for a while.

'I'll look in on him tomorrow. We've been mates since school, and he comes out on the boat and lends a hand when he hasn't got anything else on. Although he *made* more work than he saved this time!'

Susannah and Silvio had agreed it was only fair they should fill Sam in on a little of their history, because neither had been forthcoming about the police wanting them. They gave Sam the gist of their situation, concluding by saying that they had come to the coast for a relaxing break.

Sam burst out laughing. 'Sorry, I know what you've told me is very sad and serious. But your relaxing break sure didn't happen.' Silvio grinned and Susannah nodded in agreement. 'Anyway, aside from wanting to thank you properly for all your help, I wanted to give you a refund on the trip. I've already been in touch with the Welches and organised theirs and I refunded Mel at the office after the police dropped us off. So, give me your bank details and I'll sort out your refund. You never saw a dolphin, after all.'

Susannah laughed. '*You* should be paying us. A long night in the rain with no food wasn't advertised as part of your deal.'

'No. And I'm really grateful for all your help.'

There was a pause while they ate. 'Well, I don't want a refund,' Silvio said after a drink. 'I think Susannah and I came to a lot of important realisations on that disastrous cruise. Not just important in the short-term, but in a life-changing way.' He stumbled a bit with his words, then went on, 'We both grew up a heck of a lot. We realised we can rely on each other in a crisis. We woke up to how immature it was to run away from our situation on the farm. Maybe,' he added with a shy glance at Susannah, 'we realised we're very well suited to a long future together.'

Susannah blushed and looked at her plate. Then she looked up, first at Sam and then at Silvio. 'I agree with Sil. I don't think we'd have done any growing up, lolling on the beach and eating and drinking our heads off. This has been good for us in many ways. I don't want you to give us a refund either. I mean, aside from jolting us into a bit of maturity, it didn't do us a lot of harm, probably made us count our blessings more than anything else. But you, you've lost your boat, your livelihood. You're much worse off than us.'

'I'm flexible. The boat was insured. I've had plenty of different jobs. Probably time to try my hand at something else,' Sam said easily. 'If you really think the benefits of the trip outweigh the harm, then I'm glad.'

'If you want a "tree change" while you make up your mind about your next move, you're welcome to stay on the farm for a bit. See how we live in the country,' Susannah smiled. Silvio nodded.

'We're for an early night. Setting off home tomorrow,' he said draining his beer. 'You're probably dead on your feet too, Sam'

'Reckon. Anyway, I've got your number. I'll remember your offer. Maybe I could try my hand at this horse business or a spot of market gardening.'

'Great idea,' Silvio said.

CHAPTER TWENTY-FOUR

Kevin and Darren made it to Legal Aid within Ben's ninety minutes. Now that he was sure of Darren's support, Kevin was determined get the whole mess sorted out in the best and quickest way. They found Bevan Thornton, a short, serious-faced man with sandy hair. He listened carefully to Kevin's initial brief account.

'Right, let's just pause there while I call the police station and let them know you haven't done a runner,' he said.

Kevin paled at the casual words. He was horrified to think that if anything had held him up getting into town, it would immediately be assumed he had absconded.

As he ended the call, Bevan pulled a notepad towards him and said briefly, 'Begin.'

After some time of questioning and making notes of Kevin's answers, he laid his pen down. He spread his hands on the table and looked at them while he thought in silence. Kevin and Darren watched, hating the suspense.

At last Bevan seemed to have finished considering Kevin's words. 'I think,' he said, 'with nothing previous on your record, there can be no problem with you getting bail. It might be a bit steep, because the police take a dim view of interfering with a corpse. You will probably have to undertake to abide by a few restrictions like not going interstate or overseas but I'm pretty sure we can organise things so you can continue working at the stud, *if they'll have you*, until this comes to court.'

'I hadn't thought about whether I could keep my job,' Kevin faltered dejectedly.

'It'll be all right,' Darren said determinedly. 'If Dad kicks up a fuss, I'll speak up for you. We need all the staff we can hold onto just now. Remember, Hamish is gone, and we don't know when Ali will be back, not to mention Susannah. We've a lot of preparation to do for the sales. They'd be mad not to want you to stay. But to be honest, I reckon it will be more up to Jarred than Dad because Dad seems to have completely lost interest in the whole farm.'

Later, Kevin and Darren drove soberly back to the stud. To their great relief, the police had agreed to bail with, as Bevan had predicted, several restrictions.

'I guess we'd better face the music,' Kevin said reluctantly. There seemed so many hurdles to face but at least Bevan had been right in thinking Kevin could get bail. Now, he had to find out if he still had a job.

'Dad?' Darren called, heading towards his father's office. 'He's not here. Probably down at the stables.'

They found Jarred and Taj hard at work but no sign of Gordon.

'He drove off shortly after you two left,' Jarred said.

'Well, you're the manager. You can decide,' Darren said.

'As yet, I'm not sure *what* I'm deciding,' Jarred's voice was weary. He mentally abandoned any hope of getting more work done. There were too many interruptions and too few staff. 'Let's go to my office.'

Kevin was determined to have everything out in the open, so he told his tale in truthful detail.

Jarred listened in shocked silence. Finally, Kevin leant back in his chair and said, 'So that's it. You know the lot.'

'To be honest, there are a few things you two need to know as well,' Jarred felt reluctant to tell Mac's news instead of letting Mac tell it, but reasoned that since he was the manager, it was ok. He relayed the gist of his earlier conversation with Mac, watching the reactions on Kevin and Darren's faces. Kevin stared back in silence.

'God!' Darren said. 'God,' he repeated, 'What the hell else is there left to find out *now*? What a day! I don't know if I can take much more in.'

'I agree,' Jarred said. 'Do you know where your father went?'

'I'll ring him.' Darren pulled out his phone and listened to the message saying the phone was switched off. 'No answer.'

Jarred sighed. He felt like throwing up his hands and walking off. Life on the stud these days was like being tossed around in a boat without a rudder. Every day brought a new set of problems, and everything was changing too fast. His head was spinning. He thought for a few seconds.

'Look, Kevin. If the police think its ok to bail you, I'm happy to let you stay on here. Of course, the last word will be Mac's, but I reckon he'll agree with us all. Bottom line is, we need the staff. I'd rather have *you* here, than have to train someone to do your job.'

Mac stuck his head in the door. 'I thought we had work to do,' he commented in mild reproach.

'I think we'll just give up on the rest of the day,' Jarred gave a resigned sigh. 'Wait until you hear this, Mac.'

* * *

Next morning, after sharing coffee and croissants, Antonia used unavoidable appointments as an excuse for leaving Gordon to his own devices.

'I'm a big boy, I've got plenty to go on with. You carry on and I'll see you for dinner tonight. Does that suit?'

'Sounds great. I'll book us into a nice Chinese place I know in Bennet Street. Good idea?'.

Gordon nodded, walked her to the door and kissed her goodbye. Both felt they were playing their parts admirably, sure that neither knew the other's behaviour was an act.

He poured himself another coffee and set his mind to work. He had said "business commitments" would be occupying him in Perth because he didn't want Antonia to suspect his finances were under such serious threat. When he first met her, Gordon had lied, hinting at a shared interest in Divine Hayfields rather than admitting Felicity's outright ownership. He had naively discussed his betting syndicate with her, failing to appreciate that as a business lawyer, she would be fully aware of how close to the edge of legal his scheme was. He figured Antonia would not view him as her social equal and therefore not worth her time if she knew his current situation. For the next year at least, it was vital that their relationship continue to grow. If it eventually foundered, he hoped to have made enough contacts through his association with her to be able to flourish independently in the Perth business world. He realistically understood that Antonia may not want to wait around for him to extricate himself from his eastern commitments. *Just give me twelve months,* he thought grimly. And for God's sake, let those damned police fix on someone to blame for Felicity's death or bury the whole case. He didn't like to focus too much on the implications of the investigation. His thoughts centred exclusively on the time it was taking to close the case. The sooner it was closed the happier he would be. The slow progress so far made him more confident each day that they would be unable to solve the case and he could move on.

While back east, he had continued to keep a sharp eye on his syndicate via the internet and his phone. He had maintained his careful practice of laying bets and keeping track of who was current with ongoing deposits and who needed chasing for payment. His skimmings from the syndicate were growing steadily. He was beginning to feel optimistic about the money being the rescue fund he needed. He felt confident of being able to make a fresh start in Perth. He hoped news of Felicity's murder hadn't filtered across the country to sully his name. He knew he was well-qualified for a range of employment in the equine world. Gordon thought resignedly, *it would be a step down to be actually on a payroll,* but he believed he would soon re-establish himself. He had never considered the salary he drew at Divine Hayfields as such. Rather, he believed it was his rightful reward for keeping Felicity in check.

He had decided during the flight to Perth that he would use his time to expand the list of members in the syndicate. He knew he would have to spend time with Linda. She would want to know all the details of the situation on Divine Hayfields. *Scatter-brained she may be, but she has a genuine affection for her niece and nephew and is always interested to hear news of them. Well,* he thought dourly, *I've got plenty of news to share with her.* He wondered briefly what Susannah was up to. Then he shrugged. *If she wants to play about with that gardener's son, good luck to her. She and Darren are adults after all, they are both capable of making their own decisions,* he thought callously. He doubted any words of his would change their minds about the choices they made. He felt wholly ready to cut all his ties in eastern Australia. He briefly contemplated changing his name as part of his fresh start but abandoned the idea as melodramatic and unnecessary.

It felt good to be away from Divine Hayfields and the stress that seemed to spread to every corner of the place. *A quiet clean passing in her sleep would have made Felicity's death easier but that damned pitchfork has brought the police running and they just won't let up.* Gordon gave himself a mental shake to dispel the unproductive thoughts.

Instead, he dwelled for a while on the pleasurable prospect of going to the races on the weekend. He was looking forward to socialising, to being among the rich and well-connected. He enjoyed everything about being at the races, the sense of excitement among the crowd, the jostle at the bookie's windows, the thunderous sound of the thoroughbred hooves on the turf and then the sense of superiority returning to the executive box to enjoy champagne and canapes away from the common crowd. He knew he and Antonia made a handsome couple and he anticipated many useful introductions. *Ah well, time to get on,* he mused, opening the laptop.

A very different anticipation of a day at the races evolved between Antonia and Logan later when he rang her at the office.

'Don't bother booking a table in the Director's Lounge. I've already done it,' he said, nonchalantly skipping a greeting.

'Oh, that's handy,' she said tartly. His brashness got on her nerves at times. 'Something less for me to do. What time will you be getting there?'

'I shouldn't think much earlier than midday. Lunch will be laid on and we can eat round one. I've set up the action for just before race three. If Gordon doesn't seem likely to be going down to the bookies, we'll have to get him down to the parade ring before the race. My horse Perrachase is running in that race, so I'll have a good reason to ask him to go with me to see that the trainer has got her in good order. Just need to get him out of the lounge on some pretext, don't want things happening up there and causing a stink.'

'Good Heavens, no! I enjoy going to the races. I couldn't bear to get kicked out because of Gordon,' Antonia agreed fervently. 'That plan sounds workable. By the way,' she reminded him, 'I probably don't want to know the details of what you have planned. The less I know, the more genuine my reaction will be to any interested observers if I have to have a reaction.'

'Don't worry, sweetheart, I'll spare your delicate senses,' Logan chortled irreverently. Antonia could imagine him rubbing his hands gleefully in anticipation of Gordon's downfall, the profit, and, she suspected, the idea of the action. She thought disdainfully that Logan relished a bit of dirty work whereas she preferred not to dwell on the unpleasant aspects of Logan's schemes, lucrative though they always were.

Homeward bound, Susannah and Silvio navigated carefully up the mountainous road, dodging fallen branches and debris. Once or twice, they were stopped by road crews removing larger trees. They drove into Muswellbrook early afternoon and stopped at the police station.

Ben walked them into his office. He didn't appear any the worse for the car accident, but when Susannah asked after Kaylee, he said she'd be in hospital for a couple of days with broken ribs and concussion.

'Now, down to business,' he said firmly. Susannah and Silvio listened, spellbound, as Ben recounted developments.

'Huh! I can't imagine my little bro having the nerve to bash a policeman,' Susannah said.

'He kept his thing with Kevin very quiet, didn't he,' Silvio commented.

'So let me get this straight,' Susannah said. She paused, then followed her thoughts. 'I don't want to talk or even think about what Kevin did.' She shuddered. 'But so long as what he said was right about Mum already being gone when he found her, I guess I can come to terms with it. I might have to, if he and Dar make a go of their hook-up,' she smiled wryly. 'So, Dar bashed you. Are you charging him?'

'I'd say they were pretty extenuating circumstances. I hardly think he will make a habit of such violence. So, no, we won't be charging him,' Ben said dryly.

'Ok. What about Kevin?'

'The police bailed him yesterday. Last I heard, he and Darren were going back to Divine Hayfields to make a full confession and see if he still has a job.'

'And the whole investigation?' Susannah was impatient to be updated so she and Silvio could continue out to the farm.

'I think we're very close to a solution. It seems now that, your mum's anticoagulant injections were tampered with. Someone added a poisonous liquid to the needles, smeared it on. Not all the needles, about half of them. That way, your mum could have died after any random injection, not on a specific day. The poison was derived from castor oil plants. Kaylee found some in that fenced-off area your parents were working on. We missed fingerprinting your father and the housekeeper. We'll be doing that soon. We'll also be organising a search warrant to see if we can find a cache of the remains of the poison anywhere.'

Susannah sat back while she processed that news. Dad? Dell Sullivan? Who else could have got into Mum's bedroom to tamper with the needles? 'What if it's not Dad or Dell?' she asked quietly.

'We'll keep looking. The fingerprint we managed to get doesn't match any of the prints we've taken from anybody so far. It's just a process of elimination now.' There was a brief silence.

'Oh, wait a minute!' Ben slapped his forehead in frustration. 'We didn't get yours and Silvio's either!'

'Jeez!' Susannah reached for Silvio's hand. 'Well, at least you can do us now. That'll get us out of the way.'

Susannah was silent through the fingerprinting, her mind a whirl of questions and no answers. As they stood to leave the station, she said to Ben, 'This is all too much. I just want to go home. I'm so confused and sick of all the unanswered questions.'

'There's nothing more we can do to help?' Silvio looked diffidently at Ben.

'No, Silvio. I'm glad you two made it back safely. I can certainly understand you're both keen to get home, speak to your parents. But for God's sake, if you feel like buzzing off anywhere else, can you please tell us!'

'We're not going anywhere until Mum's murder is cleared up,' Susannah said firmly.

CHAPTER TWENTY-FIVE

They drove out to Wheeler, each absorbed in their thoughts. As they turned right in the village, Susannah noticed smoke rising ahead.

Fire! A dreaded part of rural Australian life. As they neared Croham, Susannah and Silvio became increasingly nervous. Their fears were confirmed as they turned in between the dramatic lion-topped pillars.

'The back paddock!' Silvio exclaimed as he leapt from the car.

Gisella burst from the front door, the usual whirlwind of colour, her eyes brimming with anxious tears.

'Oh Dio, Cara! You back! There's fire.' Her arms waved wildly.

'Shh, Mama, shh. Relax, we're here now. Shh, Mama.' He held her in a strong embrace, meeting Susannah's eyes over his mother's head.

'Zanna darling, take Mama inside. Give her a drink. I'll take the bike out and see if Dad needs a hand. Keep your phone with you in case we need help.'

She nodded. She took Gisella firmly by the arm and led her back into the house. Like Burt had done when he and Gisella discovered Silvio and Susannah were missing, she poured a large sherry. She gently pushed Gisella into the lounge and put the glass in her hand.

'Drink, Gisella. It will calm you. Burt and Silvio will be ok. If they can't cope, Silvio will call. Come on, relax.'

Whether it was the sherry or Susannah's calm words or a bit of both, Gisella subsided. As she sipped, she gazed at Susannah. Gradually, her panic abated. She gave Susannah a wavering smile. 'So, where you take my son, so I and his father have so much worry?'

Realising she could divert Gisella's hysteria, Susannah was only too happy to talk about their trip to the coast. Gisella was captivated by what she saw as a romantic getaway, despite the worry it had initially caused. Susannah began to relax, talking easily with the vivacious woman. She figured she might as well start getting better acquainted with Silvio's mother, now that she and Silvio were together. She realised that since her mum's death, she had missed a woman's company even though she and her mother had not had an easy relationship. Despite her volatile nature, Gisella was basically a warm and kind woman. Susannah hoped they could get on with each other.

She was beginning to recognise that keeping their trip a secret from the family had in a way added to her own stress, rather than relieving it. Talking about Port Macquarie, she was careful to make light of their disastrous cruise, dwelling more on their cold and hungry state rather than going into detail about the swim to safety and the boat wreck. She made much of their beach walks, their leisurely meals together, their enjoyment of window-shopping.

'Ahh, so good to be young and in love,' Gisella sighed.

Susannah felt uncomfortable. 'We're very sorry we gave you so much worry, we just wanted to get away.'

'Ahh, that! Pfft. All over now,' Gisella said grandly.

She began picturing the future out loud. Daydreaming with misty eyes, planning the wedding ceremony, the wedding feast, the guest list, the honeymoon, where the newlyweds would live, imaging the "bambinos". Susannah listened in growing horror. How would she and Sil *ever* be able to plan a life together for themselves? Who said anything about a wedding? Let alone babies! She wondered in desperation how to stop the flow of fantasies. Then her good sense asserted itself. Gisella daydreaming about the future was far preferable to Gisella panicking about the present danger of fire. Zanna decided that Gisella would forget half the plans she was making when a fresh event diverted her. She let Gisella run on, listening with half an ear, while the other was tuned for the sound of Silvio's bike returning.

Gradually Gisella's spate of happy schemes slowed. Before she could rise again to panic, Susannah asked matter-of-factly what Burt was doing.

'He say burn-off. I think not really right time of the year but he shout, he insist. Very cranky man these days.'

'Well, I'm sure Burt is too experienced to do anything silly, Gisella. Silvio will give him a hand and they'll call us if they need help.' Susannah wondered guiltily if worry about Silvio was making Burt cranky. 'Is there something you were doing that I can help you with?'

'No, you sweet girl. You sit here with me, we talk, relax. Pour me another drink, have one with me.' She patted the lounge beside her invitingly. Susannah obediently poured another large one for Gisella and a much smaller one for herself. She was not fond of sherry at the best of times. Her heart quailed as she anticipated another flood of Gisella's excited plans. This was a part of her life with Silvio that she hadn't envisaged. She would have to be a strong woman to resist Gisella's well-intentioned interference, if she and Silvio were going to make a life together on their own terms!

Silvio gunned the little ag-bike up the rutted track to the back paddock. What the hell was his father doing burning at this time of the year? He was sure they had done all the necessary hazard reduction back in Autumn.

He crested the rise and saw his father calmly driving the tractor round a small patch of blazing paddock, spraying a saturating firebreak as he went. He was clearly concentrating on what he was doing, but he seemed unworried. There was no sign that the fire was out of control but to Silvio it seemed weird, almost pointless to be burning such a clearly defined and relatively small area. And then he smelt it. *Good grief! My dad had a dope crop and he's burning it! Why burn it? What a waste!* All these thoughts chased each other round his brain, and he stared, fascinated.

His father looked up, and Silvio waved automatically. Burt's horrified reaction was almost comical. He jammed on the brakes, then jerked the tractor forward again, then stopped again. Silvio rode across to the tractor.

'Dad!'

'Go away, damn you! What the 'ell are you doing up 'ere?' Burt growled fiercely.

Silvio felt he might have the upper hand here, so he responded abruptly, 'What the hell are *you* doing, more to the point?'

Burt started blustering, one anxious eye on his son and the other on the fire.

Silvio took pity on his dad. 'Here, let's get this fire out and then you can explain why you'd be burning what looks like a perfectly good dope crop.'

Burt jumped. 'Geez, son!'

'Come on, dad. It looks like its nearly all burnt. Let's mop up the last of it and you can tell me all about it.'

Half an hour later, they both smelt of the sickly smoke, faces and clothes smudged with black soot. They sat companionably on a log watching the last whisps of smoke rising slowly. Their conversation had ranged from the crop, the fire and the reason for the fire to Silvio's trip to the coast, to Felicity's murder, to Susannah. It seemed they felt more at ease with each other at this moment than they had in many previous months.

'Holy hell!' Silvio leant back on the log. He looked at his dad, then his face cracked into a wide grin. He threw back his head and let out a roar of laughter. Burt looked at his son, stunned. Then his face relaxed, he grinned. Soon they were both laughing together, tears running down their faces. All the recent stress, anxiety, and relief poured out together, convulsing them with laughter. Gradually they calmed down, took a breath and checked the fire. All that remained was hot ash.

'I'll give it one more wetting and then it's time to start workin' on our story. Your mum was a bit suspicious about me 'aving the fire.'

'She was pretty worked up when Zanna and I arrived, that's for sure! Lucky we got there when we did, she could have *really* panicked and rang the fire service!' Silvio looked guilty. 'I feel bad leaving Zanna with Mama like that. But I guess she needs to learn that's part of life with me!'

'Girl sounds pretty strong an' sensible from what you've just said, son. An' you're right, she'll need to get used to your mum's hot-blooded nature. By crikey, it'll do her a power of good to 'ave a female about.' He looked slyly at Silvio, 'Might take the 'eat off you an' me a bit, eh son?'

Silvio grinned again. 'You drive round the fire, and I'll hold the hose, and we'll be done. I'm looking forward to a beer, it's been a long day ... long few days, to be honest. Come on.'

They arrived back at the house to find Gisella very mellow. In the kitchen, Silvio gave Susannah a brief rundown while she was getting beers and putting out a few snacks. As she heard the details, her eyes grew rounder and rounder. Finally, she looked at him and started giggling.

'Oh, don't get me started again,' Silvio groaned, grinning. She struggled to stifle the laughter.

'This is so ridiculous! The police letting your dad off and him having to watch his crop go up in smoke. It's a wonder he wasn't crying when you turned up! Oh heck, I really do need a drink, now that I know you're safe and the fire crisis, dope crop,' she giggled again, 'is all over. What a crazy anticlimax to all the recent stresses!'

'Will we stay here tonight?' Silvio asked as she handed

him a plate of snacks to take in to his parents. She looked at him, thinking.

'Maybe you stay here with your folks and catch them up on everything. I told your mum a bit but kept it low-key so she wouldn't get upset. I'll go home tonight and do the same with Dad and Dar. Then maybe tomorrow, we'll have a barbie together at home or something and we can all make a few decisions about how we go on from here.'

He nodded slowly. Susannah added firmly, 'But you hear this Silvio Bunrack, we have done our time of sneaking round! From now on we're together and open about it no matter where we sleep each night.'

He hugged her hard saying simply, 'Ti amo.' She felt a little thrill at the intimate, softly spoken words. They shared a long kiss.

'You know, sweetheart, I reckon we've both grown up a few *years* in the last few days! But let's not allow all this new maturity to stop us from enjoying ourselves like young people should.'

He kissed her again, 'We'll be fine, little love.'

Susannah used the short drive home in the dusk to try to get her thoughts in order. She was dreading her father's reaction to the news about her and Silvio. She knew, also, he would be very critical of their decision to go away without letting anyone know. She squared her shoulders resolutely and sighed sadly. It was so hard to comprehend her mum was dead, no longer an enormous presence on the farm. Susannah knew she would forever miss her mother's opinion, but she sensibly recognised that she could comfortably live without the criticism and the domineering.

She drove along the sweeping drive feeling the familiar sense of security of being home. As far as she could see the barn was settled and still for the night, although she knew Jarred would do a last walk around after his supper, just to be sure everything was right for the night. She guessed he'd be doing that without fail from now on, without her mum around keep an eye on things.

'I'm home,' she yelled, walking into the kitchen. 'Anyone about?'

Darren came out of his room. 'Hey, you. Welcome back to Divine Hayfields, house of never-ending drama.' His expression was a mixture of cynicism and pleasure.

'Hey, Dar. How are you? I'm sorry I haven't been here for you, just left you with the lot. Where's Dad?' She hugged him tight.

'I'm coping. Can't really believe the whirlwind life here has become. As for Dad, I would *guess* he's gone to Perth, but I don't know for sure because he's not answering his phone. And that'll *really* please the police, NOT! They were mad enough that you and Silvio cleared-off without telling them.'

Susannah laughed guiltily and hugged her brother again. 'That'd be right, clearing-off back to Perth! Well, little bro, we have a bit of catching up to do. Have you eaten?'

'Ahh,' Darren looked embarrassed. Then he rushed on, 'Kevin and I were just going to heat up a couple of frozen dinners.'

Susannah tried to keep her face bland while thinking how quickly Darren had moved his lover in.

'Is there enough for three?' she asked neutrally. 'I had a

few drinks at Silvio's, but I'm starving, and I feel like *really* unwinding. We could have a bottle of wine or two with it.'

'Are you ok for Kevin to stay and eat with us?' Darren asked shyly.

'Dear little bro, we've both been through the mill lately. If you have someone to love and comfort you, I'm happy for you,' she said honestly. 'I think you and I will find ourselves depending on each other a lot more without Mum and with Dad apparently happier in Perth.'

'We'll work it out, Sis. If this makes us appreciate each other more, that's got to be a good thing, right?'

'Indeed. Let's the three of us just have a relaxing meal and a few drinks tonight. We've got a lot to catch each other up on. If Kevin is part of your life now, I have no problem with him being here. You'll soon have to get used to having Silvio included in my world.'

After some initial awkwardness and embarrassment, the wine loosened their nervousness. Kevin was initially reserved about intruding on the conversation. He thought this was all private family stuff and was diffident about joining in. Susannah and Darren included him easily and he gradually relaxed and began to take part. There was indeed plenty to relate to each other, so many things had happened since Susannah had gone to the coast. They ate the packaged dinners, which Susannah had improved by adding garlic bread and salad.

Later that evening, they discussed the most pressing issues. Recent events had been emotionally draining for them all and it was an intense relief to share the load. Susannah suddenly laughed and decided Burt's fire would make a light-hearted topic to end the evening. It was the perfect remedy after so many difficult revelations.

The laughter when she finished the tale threatened to engulf them all the way it had Silvio and Burt.

'Poor old Burt, having to burn his dope,' Darren said regretfully. 'I was the one who dobbed him in, I'm afraid. I'm no good at keeping secrets.'

'I want to have a barbie, one evening soon, with Silvio and his folks. We probably need to let them know the changes here. Do we leave it to Mac to let everyone know he's our half-brother and the stud's new owner?'

'We'll talk to him tomorrow. Have to let him decide how much of what's basically our business he wants shared round the district. Because you can rest assured once it is common knowledge here on the farm, its common knowledge in the district.' Darren spoke reasonably.

'This has got to be the reason Dad disappeared. I'm sure he assumed he would inherit, or at least you and I would.'

'After you and Silvio left, he was in a thunderous mood the whole time. But you two leaving happened pretty much at the same time he went to the solicitors. So, you're probably right. It is all so complicated. How do you feel about a half-brother you never knew about?'

'Just another amazing fact to come to terms with. You realise this means you're an uncle now?' she chuckled.

'You're an aunt,' he countered.

Susannah drained her glass. 'I guess we should all sleep on it. With Dad obviously deciding Perth is his priority, we'll have to get used to discussing everything with Mac and Jarred. Are they happy for you to keep working here, Kevin?'

'Yeah,' he said pausing uncomfortably. 'I just want you both to know how truly sorry I am for my actions the night your Mum died. I behaved so terribly ...'

Darren put his arm protectively around Kevin's shoulder, waiting for Susannah's reaction.

She sighed sadly. 'Look, Kevin. What's done is done. We just *have* to move on. We can't change anything. I think if we're going to all be part of each other's lives, we need to learn to trust and accept each other and make the best of things.'

Kevin's eyes shone with grateful tears. 'Thanks, Susannah. That means a lot.'

She stood up and gave them both a hug. 'I'm done in. My last holiday wasn't exactly restful! Rest up, you two, I'd say we've got another big day ahead of us.'

CHAPTER TWENTY-SIX

Susannah and Darren asked Mac to come up to the house for lunch the next day. The outcome of that meeting was that Susannah and Gisella would organise an informal evening, inviting several of the closer neighbours and other people from the village so Mac could announce his ownership of Divine Hayfields in his own way. Mac felt nervous and ill-at-ease, very unsure of himself in his new role. He gathered his confidence and said he wanted to start in way he intended to go on, with openness and honesty. Susannah was at pains to help make his transition as smooth as possible.

'Did you know your dad has threatened to contest the will?'

'Oh no!' Susannah exclaimed. 'Not more complications. Oh, that would be too horrible!'

'If we have to, we'll cross that bridge when we come to it,' Mac said. 'Are you both staying on to work for me? Or would you prefer to move on? I know it's tricky as this is your family home. You need to know I'm staying where I am for the time being because I want life to remain as stable as possible for my son. Besides, it is very convenient for Nadia's work and the school and Jack's grandparents being so close together. We can work the finer details out further down the track.'

'Of course, little Jack! Yes, I can imagine you want to keep life on an even keel for him. I can't believe I'm his aunty!' Susannah said, happily diverted to a less serious topic.

'Didn't the solicitor say things had to go on the same for a bit?' Darren asked diffidently.

'Yeah, why?'

'Well, we don't really need to make any decisions right now, do we? I personally have had about as much change as I can take for now,' Darren said emphatically. 'I'm happy to stay right here doing my job.'

To Mac's intense relief, Susannah agreed.

Mac began to feel hopeful that they could continue the program of preparation for the sales without making any changes. The stock agent had located an extra hand who had some experience with horses. Mac tasked Taj with the job of helping Danny become familiar with their routine. Danny was quick to learn, and although everyone was still extremely busy, life at Divine Hayfields began to settle back into a semblance of normality. There was even time for Mac to catch up with Burt and set in motion construction of the permanent fencing round the wetland. Burt said he and Silvio would do the labour, so Mac didn't have to lose manpower on the job. Mac was gratified by the ready acceptance of his new position.

Into the relative peace, the return of the police was an unwelcome intrusion. This time it was Ben accompanied by Sergeant Rob Phelps.

'Have you got some progress to report? How's Kaylee? How are you?' Susannah was impatient for news.

'Nothing new. Kaylee's doing well. I'm fine.' Ben smiled and introduced his partner. 'We need to get fingerprints from your housekeeper.'

'Oh. I'll take you out to her.' They walked through the kitchen to the laundry. 'Dell, the police need your fingerprints.'

'For heaven's sake! Things have come to a pretty pass out here. A murder, fingerprinting! Am I a suspect?'

'Dell, we know this is inconvenient for you, but we just need to rule you out. It's merely routine and I'm sure a law-abiding citizen like yourself is all in favour of assisting the police in their enquiries.' Ben smiled his sweetest smile.

'Humph! When you put it like that, ok. I guess you'll make a mess I have to clean up.'

'No, no, Mrs Sullivan. We won't leave any mess, trust me. Hold out your hands and we'll get it over with as quickly as we can.' Ben decided the public relations course he had done a few months ago had just paid dividends.

After he had finished taking Dell's prints, Ben located Darren at his desk, while Rob put the fingerprints and equipment in the car. 'We need your father's prints, too. Is he in his office?' he asked.

Darren had been quietly enjoying having his relationship with Kevin out in the open. He felt calmer having Zanna back home sharing the load. The return to semi-normal on the farm had also helped him regain some peace of mind. He found that with the peace of mind came a degree of self-confidence he hadn't felt before.

He heard Ben's question and worried he would be nervous telling Ben he had no idea where his father was. Instead, he was philosophical, reasoning it was not his problem, he was just relaying the news.

A short silence fell. 'Well, where is he?' Ben's mouth had tightened into a grim line.

'We're guessing he's in Perth. But *only* guessing because he isn't answering calls from any of us, not Mac, not Jarred, or Zanna or me.'

'There is another thing besides the fingerprints. We have a search warrant, as well.'

'Well, I'd say, since Mac owns the place, now, you should talk to him about the warrant. He'll be down at the stables.' Darren surprised himself with his calmness.

'I've got to hand it to you, Darren,' Ben said admiringly, 'this confident attitude suits you.'

'Thanks,' Darren responded modestly. 'There had to be some good come out of this mess.'

'Yeah, I guess. See you later.' With a casual wave, Ben left for the stables. Darren watched him go, his thoughts swirling. He was pleased with Ben's encouraging words, but he was reminded again he was living in an unsolved murder and the mention of a search warrant was a jarring shock. He let out a long slow breath, he'd be so glad when this was all sorted out.

Ben was shortly back at the house, with Mac.

'What do I do, Darren?' he asked, feeling out of his depth.

'Let them look,' Darren said simply.

Ben took charge. 'Bedrooms, then office, lounge, family, kitchen, utility rooms, I think, Rob. We'll work together.

Chapter Twenty-Six

It'll take some time but that can't be helped.'

Darren went back to his desk but the significance of the sounds of the police working at their task made him feel unsettled.

'Got a minute, Darren?' Ben stuck his head round the door. 'We need to open your father's safe if you know the combination.'

Darren felt his mouth go dry. This was all so intrusive, but he reminded himself why the intrusion was necessary and felt a little better.

He went with the policemen back to his father's office where he quickly opened the safe.

'So, how many people know the combination?' Rob asked suspiciously.

'All of us, Mum, Dad, Zanna and me. The combination is all our birth dates. We only use the safe for birth certificates, passports, insurance documents, a bit of spare cash. No need to keep certificates of ownership of the horses any longer. That's all stored with Racing Australia. Supposed to cut out opportunities for the dishonest element to do a little gentle forgery. Not a bad idea, it seems to work.'

His customary flow of informative conversation was silenced by a sharp exclamation for Ben.

'Well, well, well. Just look at this!'

The colour faded from Darren's face as he took in the three small, sealed glass tubes Ben was holding up in his gloved hand.

'Oh my God!'

'Is there anything you can tell us about these, Darren?' Rob asked sternly.

'No! No, I've never seen them before.' Darren shook his head in denial. 'Do you think that's the poison that was smeared on Mum's needles?'

'Quite possibly. Can you get Susannah in here?'

Darren quickly rang Susannah's mobile. 'The police need you in Dad's office right away.'

Susannah reacted with the same adamant negative that Darren had. 'I don't think I've been near the safe in the last six months,' she added.

'We'll fingerprint these. Now look, you two, you simply *must not* leave Divine Hayfields. Darren, I know we can trust you, but Susannah, I can't stress enough how very important it is for you to stay here.' Ben spoke with heavy emphasis.

'I know, I know. My record is poor, but I *promise* I will not go anywhere until your investigation is wrapped up! I truly do understand how wrong it was for Silvio and me to go away and I assure you, it won't happen again.'

Darren moved over and put his arm round her shoulder. 'We're handling things together these days. Ben, you have my word, Zanna and I will stay here.'

Susannah was grateful for Darren's loyal support and told him so while they shared a coffee after the police departed.

'What do you think about that stuff in the safe?'

'No idea,' Darren said soberly. 'But if you didn't put it there and I didn't put it there, what are we left with? I can't see Mum mucking round with poison vials ...'

They looked at each other in horror.

'Let's not speculate anymore!' Susannah said hastily. 'I

can't bear to think about it!'

In Perth, Logan Kirby was on the telephone.

'Got a job for a couple of willing blokes. No names, solid cash for a solid job.'

'When?'

'Saturday, at the races, just before race three. Nothing too public, but nothing so hidden away that the victim remains undiscovered. We've got to have police and ambulance, all the bells and whistles. The job might take a little time. I want some info. He might be resistant. Your choice whether you bash him to get the info or bash him to thank him for the info. So, to put it simply, two things: a bashing and some info. He *has to* get the message that his activities are a no-go zone in Perth. But I don't want him killed, so be careful. Probably best if he can't give a clear description of his attackers, too. You got anyone in mind?'

'Reckon I could stand a bit of action myself. Things have been a bit quiet lately. I've got a nice beard that is just about ready to come off, the way the missus has been nagging me about it. I can think of a handy assistant who enjoys a bit of a scrap. He doesn't mind swapping from fair hair to dark and back again.' The drawling voice sharpened a little, 'Give me details.'

'Guy by the name of Gordon Hathaway. Pretty solidly built, so you'll have to be on your game. Get on the internet, look up Divine Hayfields horse stud and you'll see his picture there as being, quote, "one of the team".' Logan couldn't keep the sneer out of his voice.

He went on, 'I need his syndicate web address and password. I also need his phone and password. He's horning in on a bit of my business and I want it stopped. I don't mind if he gets a few scars, but I don't want him dead, remember.'

'I hear you. How do I get my money?'

'I'll meet you at the usual pub in Queen Street, Monday lunch time. Payment on receipt of phone, accuracy of info and number of bruises.'

'Don't worry, he'll be bruised, mate!'

The call was ended with both parties satisfied.

Gordon exercised all his considerable charm extending the syndicate list. He visited Linda and picked over her address book, scrounging for more names willing to be in on the deal. His thoughts swung between anticipation of a day at the races and cautious optimism about the success of his syndicate. Since switching his phone back on after his flight to Perth, he had refused to answer any calls from back east. Any calls from unknown numbers also went unanswered as usual. He was meticulous recording the numbers and names of all new syndicate members making sure not to miss answering any of their calls. Everyone else could wait or rot, as far as he was concerned.

He idled away some time in pleasant reveries about his future in Perth. It wasn't difficult faking his enthusiasm for Antonia because she *was* very attractive and easy to get along with. Her wealth and high profile in the Perth business world were added bonuses. *Was she a little remote this time, or is my imagination working overtime?* he wondered with a twinge of unease.

With the end of her farcical relationship in sight, Antonia felt increasingly impatient for it to be over. *A pity the whole thing is a set-up,* she mused, *Gordon is very easy on the eye, and generous too.* She wrinkled her nose then, reminding herself how utterly boring he was. *Yeah,* she thought, *I couldn't be bothered schooling him to be less self-centred, better off without him. But maybe it's time I started looking a little more seriously for someone. I'm not getting any younger.* She shrugged. *I might do a little quiet research on Saturday while Gordon is having fun with Logan,* she concluded coldly.

CHAPTER TWENTY-SEVEN

Ben strolled along the hospital corridor, screwing up his nose at the familiar disinfectant smell.

'Well, here's a breath of fresh air!' Kaylee couldn't keep the relief from her voice. She was feeling much better and extremely bored by the lack of activity.

'Hi'ya. Ready for a bit of news?'

'Yes! No! This means you've solved it without me! That's just too bad,' she wailed.

'Relax. It's not solved, but we *have* made progress. We went out to the stud, fingerprinted the housekeeper. She wasn't happy. But we've ruled her out. We took the search warrant with us, too. Just guess what we found in the safe! In the *safe*, mind you, that *all four* of the Hathaways have easy access to!'

'Poison? Couldn't be! That's too easy.'

'And just guess who has disappeared and is not answering his phone!'

'Stop playing around! You obviously feel very clever but it's not fair to make me play twenty questions!'

Ben couldn't help relishing his moment of glory, but he took pity on Kaylee.

'Gordon has gone. We are all assuming he's in Perth but

he's not answering his phone. In the safe, we found three sealed vials, full of poison. The fingerprints on those vials don't match those of any we have taken so far. So probably not planted by someone else. We've checked the database, but Gordon has no record, so no luck matching him that way. It is beginning to look very much as if it was Gordon who doctored the needles randomly so there was a chance Felicity would use a doctored one while he was away and he wouldn't be implicated. A fairly naïve plan and easy to shoot holes in with a bit of diligent policing. I guess he kept the excess poison for another go if the first attempt failed. Imagine being so dumb as to leave the stuff in the safe! Especially since they all know the combination, although Susannah said she probably hadn't been near the safe in months. We've got Sydney airport police checking for Gordon's car in the long-term carpark. I'm going to ring Perth police when I get back to the office, assuming we have a positive response from Sydney airport.'

'Well! Gordon? Wow!'

'Yeah, looks like it. How much longer do we have to carry the load for you, slacker?'

'With luck, tomorrow. You'll still be carrying the load though, 'cos I'll only be on light duties,' she chuckled.

It's a slow process working with police from another state, so the search for Gordon in Western Australia did not proceed with lightening swiftness. He continued pursuing his interests in Perth, oblivious of the fact that he was wanted by New South Wales police regarding his wife's murder.

Antonia pleaded an unavoidable work commitment

for the evening before the races and excused herself from staying at the hotel with Gordon. On race day, he arranged to make his own way to Ascot racecourse and meet her there at noon. He dressed carefully, enjoying pleasurable anticipation that he always felt when wearing his dress suit. He tried but failed to keep his excitement in check. Antonia had mentioned inviting an associate to join them, and he mused over meeting the associate and possibly many other useful people.

Gordon arrived early and had the taxi drop him at gate one. He wanted to stroll all the way through the racecourse complex, familiarising himself with the layout, breathing in the excited mood of the growing crowd. He located the parade ring, mounting yard, horse stalls and the bookie's stands. From there he walked out onto the wide lawn and down to the rail. He leant there for a moment, allowing himself to dream of the day when all this was familiar and easily accessible. He watched the colourful mob thronging cheerfully to their chosen vantage points. At last, he made his way up to the Director's Lounge drinking in every opulent detail as he went.

'Gordon.' Antonia greeted him, kissing his cheek coolly when he walked over to where she and Logan were already at a table. 'I'd like you to meet Logan Kirby.'

They shook hands and exchanged the usual social pleasantries of people meeting for the first time. Logan lost no time letting Gordon know he had a horse running in the third race, offering to take him down to the mounting yard to meet the trainer. He was very proud to be an owner and loved showing off his horses to anyone who showed the slightest interest. Gordon was equally happy to accept the offer, knowing he would be introduced to more worthwhile contacts in the process.

'Are you a betting man?'

'I'm very much hands-on with all aspects of horse racing, from breeding to betting,' Gordon replied expansively. 'At the stud, I love the excitement of the birth of a potential racer, watching it grow from all wobbly legs into a well-balanced beautiful creature. I relish the challenge of preparing for the yearling sales. At the races, I enjoy the hustle and bustle of the bookie's windows, the sound of the horses rushing to the finish, coming back up here for celebratory drinks. *All* of it is a heady thrill for me. Talking of drinks, Antonia, Logan, what would you like?'

He strolled over to the bar, looking every inch the confident, successful businessman. No one would suspect his finances were in a very dubious state, nor would they guess just by looking at him that Gordon was on edge. A great deal depended on him successfully getting his foot in the door of Perth's rich and influential today.

They enjoyed lunch from the all-day grazing menu. Antonia circulated with Gordon, casually introducing him to her many acquaintances who stopped to greet her. Gordon was all charm, not adding much to the conversations, the better to memorise as many details as possible about those he met.

He excused himself just before race two, to go down and "suck in the atmosphere" as he put it and place a couple of bets. Then he walked to the rail so he would feel the earth vibrate with the thunder of thoroughbred hooves charging towards the finish. He felt anonymous among the crowd, able to let down his guard and enjoy being among like-minded people. He cheered loudly along with all the other successful punters, believing it a good omen that his first bet of the day had been a winner.

After collecting from the bookies, he went back up to join Antonia and Logan. They all enjoyed a relaxed drink and Gordon congratulated them on the quality of the racecourse complex. They smiled proudly, happily accepting praise for something they had no hand in creating.

Downtown, at Perth police station, Sergeant Harris picked up a memo from the duty desk. He read the details requesting assistance from New South Wales police to locate one Gordon Hathaway, wanted for questioning in relation to his wife's murder.

'When did this come in?'

'Not sure, Sarge. Was here when I came in. I assume it's been sent out to every station. There's not much detail is there, about where we start looking. Don't those Easterners realise how big Western Australia is?'

'Apparently not,' he responded dryly. 'But at least they've sent along a nice clear picture so when he falls in our lap, we're sure to recognise him.' Little did he realise how true his joking words would turn out to be. 'Deal with it as best you can for now. On Monday, we'll have more staff and can put the wheels in motion to do what we can to locate the guy.'

Logan drained his glass and stood up. 'Going down to see Perrachase. You ready, Gordon? We'll see you in a bit, Antonia.'

They made their way down and through the crowds to the mounting yard. Logan briefly introduced Gordon to his trainer. Then he began animatedly interrupting the trainer giving last-minute instructions to the jockey and fussing with the girth. Gordon sensed the trainer's impatience with Logan's interference and took a step back, distancing himself from something that he knew he, too, would find irritating. His attention drifted from Logan to take in the overall air of controlled urgency among the men and horses.

Without warning, he felt himself being jostled away from Logan. He tried to resist the movement but a large, bearded man on his left hissed in his ear. 'Just keep moving, feller, nice and easy.'

Gordon sensed rather than saw another man on his right. He was being forced rapidly but unobtrusively away towards a wide loose hedge bordering the members' carpark. His mind was spinning. *What the hell? Is this a robbery?* He thought he might have been able to fight off one heavyweight, but not two.

In among the shrubs, he was suddenly punched in the side of the head. He reeled away from the punch to collide with another, this time in the kidneys. He groaned and belatedly tried to defend himself. Another savage punch split his lip, followed by two more in the kidneys and stomach. He fell to the ground and felt himself savagely kicked in the back and ribs. He threw out an arm to fend off the blows, but it was brutally stomped on. He tried to make himself smaller curling into a ball but couldn't avoid the kicks. Abruptly he felt himself yanked to his feet by the collar of his coat.

'Give us your phone,' the voice hissed again in his left ear. He tried to squirm around to see his attacker, but hadn't the strength left to fight against the thick, strong arms gripping him. 'Phone and password, NOW!' Gordon fumbled in his pocket, passing over the phone while mumbling, 'Four, four, two, eight, zero, zero,' through his split lip. He turned his head towards the voice and was struck viciously on the nose. Blood spurted and his eyes watered. Another punch split his eyebrow, the free-flowing blood blinding him.

'Now, the web address of your syndicate and password. Don't dick me around. I'm beginning to enjoy bashing you.' A sharp jab to the ribs emphasised the menacing words. Gordon could barely think straight through the pain in his nose. It hurt his chest to breathe. His head was pushed down, and a knee cracked into his face.

'Jesus, stop!' he groaned. In the pause, he mumbled the address and password.

'That wasn't so hard, now was it,' the voice spoke conversationally. It continued with brutal emphasis on each word, 'Now listen hard, fella: *No*,' kick in the ribs, '*more*,' knee to the groin, '*syndicating*,' punch in the face, '*horse racing*. You got that?'

Without warning he was thrust face down to the ground. A few more violent kicks and then peace at last.

'Oh God,' he moaned, his breath coming noisily through his bleeding nose. 'Oh, God.' He tried to keep his breaths shallow. Another wordless moan escaped him.

'Ooh, what's that?' A lilting lady's voice spoke close by.

'Help,' Gordon rasped.

'Oh my! Look, Fred! Look! Is he drunk?' she trilled.

Chapter Twenty-Seven

'Careful Serena, let me see.'

'I think he's hurt. Yes, he is! There's blood. Ooh, Fred! We should call the police.'

'Don't get too close to him, he might be dangerous!'

'Oh Freddy, we've had such an exciting day and now this! Quickly, call the police. We can be heroes.'

Freddy was quite happy to phone the police, but he had no intention of involving himself any further. A brief call to the authorities and then he and Serena were into their rented limousine and away. He wasn't going to waste the next stage of a fabulous day giving statements at the station just because some dumb punter got himself bashed up.

'Help me, please,' Gordon croaked feebly.

'Yeah, mate. You just be quiet, and we'll get help for you. Then we're off, so you can forget you ever saw us.'

Gordon faded in and out. He felt every bone and muscle screaming. He had never been attacked; had no idea it could feel so pitiless.

His mind drifted, confused wisps of thought chased each other through the fog of pain.

Wheels crunched on the gravel. Were the attackers back? *Oh God, I can't take any more of this,* he thought in agony.

'Over here, Sarge. Here he is, half under these bushes. Looks in bad shape. Can you hear me, sir? Don't try to move. The ambulance is on the way.'

'Good job, Jackson. Has he been robbed?'

'No, here's his wallet. Let's see who we've got here.'

'Here's the ambulance,' the Sergeant interrupted. 'You go with him, then check out his story when he's been patched up. Call me as soon as he's able to talk. D'you see any sign of the guy who made the call?'

In the Director's Lounge, Antonia raised her eyebrows as Logan strolled towards her. He nodded briefly and gestured, 'Drink?'

She nodded, smiled and mouthed, 'Bubbles.'

CHAPTER TWENTY-EIGHT

Susannah was carrying feed bags with Taj and Danny when her phone rang.

'Just so you're in the loop and to prepare you for possible bad news,' Ben started. Susannah stiffened and felt her heartrate go up. 'We've asked the Western Australia police to look for your dad. I'm afraid many things are starting to point to him being involved in your mother's death.'

'Oh no!' She willed herself to stay calm, but the words burst out. 'Oh dear. What a sad mess. And I suppose we'll soon have to deal with the media. Oh, poor Mum. She'd *hate* this. We're supposed to be introducing Mac to a few people as the new owner tonight! What do we do about this?'

'Look, Susannah,' Ben said kindly. 'Don't jump ahead too far. Let Darren and Mac and Silvio know what I've told you, but I wouldn't say anything more until you know something more. If anyone from the media contacts you, just go with the old 'No comment', and hang up. Certainly, I would say nothing to Gisella, but Silvio and Burt will know best how to deal with her.'

'Yes, that makes sense. Thanks, Ben. How's Kaylee?'

'She should be at work on light duties soon.'

'Say g'day from me, and thanks for letting me know about Dad.' She sighed heavily as she hung up the phone. She went in search of Darren.

A bored journalist was drifting unobtrusively in the Emergency waiting room of Royal Perth Hospital, hoping for a juicy crumb to fill last-minute newspaper spaces. She saw the bloodied, beaten man being brought in and hovered closer trying to hear details. She took in the man's elegant suit pants, now thoroughly smudged and dirty, and heard the words 'racecourse' and 'assault'. This was enough to encourage her that it might be worthwhile to wait round a little longer. She noted the policeman who accompanied the victim, but she didn't recognise him. If she'd known him, the chances were good she'd have been able to wheedle him into letting her interview the victim. Never mind, she shrugged, even coppers need a pit stop. She paid careful attention to the cubicle the victim was taken to and then sat down to wait. She had lingered a bare half hour when she heard the policeman's radio crackle. The constable stepped out of the cubicle where he had been waiting for the semi-conscious victim to receive treatment and listened to the message.

'Jackson, don't wait round with that guy. We can get details from the hospital later. All hell's broken at the footy. The ref apparently made an unpopular decision. They need all available hands. Get yourself down there, pronto.' Jackson was only too happy to exchange a boring wait at the hospital for some action at the football and gleefully hurried away from the hapless victim.

'What luck,' murmured the journalist, eyeing the

departing policeman. She stood up and straightened her work-jaded skirt. Putting on a concerned face, she sidled carefully into the cubicle where Gordon lay. He'd apparently been given treatment for the pain but was now awaiting further assessment. In the way of all busy emergency rooms, he'd been shunted down from top priority once it had been established his injuries weren't life threatening.

'Hey, guy,' the reporter cooed in her gentlest voice. 'Looks like you've been in the wars.'

Gordon opened his right eye; the left being completely swollen shut. He saw a lady with softly curling fair hair framing her face. She was smiling gently at him. He felt sick with relief to hear a kindly accent after all the hurried, impersonal medical questioning. He had longed for Antonia but with no phone he was lost.

'I'm Therese. How'd you get in such a mess?' She managed to convey reassurance and encouragement. Over the years, she had honed her skills in quickly setting people at ease, using a calming tone. She was also well aware that she only had a short time to get her information and scoot before she was sent packing by the hospital staff.

Gordon almost wept to hear a caring voice. He was drifting in a fog that held him just above unconscious and just below the horrible pain of his beating. He was grateful that the pain was being held at bay, but he had a strong feeling of ill-usage because no one seemed to *care* that he'd been bashed and robbed.

'Why don't you tell me your tale?' the persuasive voice went on. The combination of pain medication and relief to hear Therese's apparent concern, made the words pour out of him. His sense of injustice and loneliness made him all the more talkative. In no time, Therese was smiling like the cat that got the cream. She recorded their conversation on her phone, snapped a couple of pictures, then quickly excused herself. Checking the time, she was pleased to see she was safely within the deadline to get her snippet in tomorrow's edition.

Antonia was sipping coffee when she flicked open the morning paper. SOCIETY PUNTER BASHED AT RACES the front page screamed, complete with a terrible photo of Gordon's bruised and swollen face.

She quickly read the article, noting with relief that although Gordon was named, he hadn't mentioned her or Logan. Had simply said he was with friends in the Director's Lounge. Do I visit him in hospital? Or just drop him cold? I think I'll just forget he was ever in my life. Whatever, I'll soon be free of him.

She finished her coffee, slipped into joggers and headed for King's Park, with a spring in her step.

'Well, well, well. What have we here? Why does this face look familiar?' The Sergeant sipped his coffee, while he focused of the mangled face underneath the headlines in front of him. 'Hey, Jackson, where's that request for info that came in from the eastern states?'

'Here, Sarge.'

'Do you reckon that's our man?' Sergeant Harris took the memo and held it beside the newspaper photo, critically studying the two pictures.

Jackson let out a long slow breath. 'How about that?' he chuckled. 'You *said* he'd fall in our lap, and you were right!'

'Well, let's not get too far ahead of ourselves. He might have been discharged.'

'I'd say he'd still be in there, Sarge. He was in a pretty bad way. I'll just ring the hospital.' In short time, he hung up the phone with a brief word of thanks. 'Who's driving? You or me?'

In the uncomfortable hospital cot, Gordon had trouble believing that he truly felt *worse* this morning, despite the regular doses of pain medication. His swollen face felt tight and rigid. He was unable to breathe through his nose. The stitches on his eyebrow pulled and stung. Numerous bruises made it impossible to find relief in any position. His arm was bandaged stiffly. The ice packs on his ribs brought their own special form of discomfit. He longed for a friendly face. *Where is Antonia? Where did that nice woman from last night go?* His sense of isolation was increased by the theft of his phone. His miserable thoughts were interrupted by the arrival of Sergeant Harris and his cheerful colleague.

'Good morning. Mr Hathaway, is it?'

Gordon nodded, then winced.

'Care to tell us how you got in this shape?'

Slowly Gordon worked his split lips and dry throat. He gave a halting account of his bashing, including the theft of his phone. Even though his brain was very foggy, he realised repeating the one-sided conversation he had from his attackers would lead to further intrusive questions. Belatedly he remembered just how close to illegal his syndicate was. It dawned on him he had naively ignored the fact that he could be encroaching on somebody else's turf. He sighed inwardly.

'Did you get enough of a look at your attackers to give us a description?'

'No.'

'Ok, Mr Hathaway,' the Sergeant said conversationally. 'Now we've got that out of the way, can you tell us why you would be wanted by New South Wales police in connection with your wife's murder?'

Gordon jumped, gasped as pain shot through every part of him. *Oh God,* he thought, *oh God. Now?*

'We have a memo asking for us to look for you and low and behold you have landed in our lap. What do you have to say about any of this?'

Susannah was making a coffee. She had already been down to the stables and done her share of the feeding and mucking out. Everyone seemed more relaxed and despite still being very busy, work preparing horses for the sale was progressing well. In her pocket, her phone beeped a message. It was not from Silvio as she had anticipated. A girlfriend in Sydney had sent the message.

Your Dad is in the news. Check it out.

Susannah's heart sank. She opened the news app on her phone and began scrolling through the headlines. A low groan escaped her as she read the article.

'Dar! Dar,' she called, 'come and read this. It's just horrible. Ben said they were going to ask the Western Australian police to look for Dad. Now he's been bashed up and in the news. That'll make him easy to find. I wonder how badly he's hurt. I wish he'd answer his phone. Do you think it was a random attack?'

Darren looked up from the screen. 'He doesn't seem too

concerned about us over here if he's off at the races,' he said coldly.

'Look at the picture, he's an absolute mess.' Susannah felt close to tears. 'Do you think Ben is on the right track? Connecting Dad to Mum's murder?'

Darren answered slowly, 'I guess. I mean they reckon they've ruled out everyone else. All the WA cops have to do is fingerprint Dad and send the pictures over here. It'll be conclusive then.' He shrugged sadly. 'What a complete mess.'

'Well, little bro, if it was Dad, we are lucky we're pulling together these days. We'll be leaning on each other a lot, grieving for Mum and, I guess, for Dad too. Go down and let Jarred and Kevin know the latest. Mac was still down there when I came up, so he'll have to know too. I'll just nip over to Silvio's and let them know. I can't believe any of this. It's too awful.'

Her phone rang as she spoke.

'Wait, Darren. It's Ben.' She spoke into the phone, 'Hi, Ben. We've just seen the news ...'

'Hi Susannah. You'd better expect the worst now in terms of publicity, I'm afraid. Stick with 'No comment' for as long as you can. The WA police are going to fingerprint your dad while he's still in hospital to speed things along.'

'How *is* Dad? Is he badly hurt? Was it a random attack or has he got into some trouble in Perth, too?'

'It seems to have been a pretty comprehensive bashing. His nose is broken, stitches in the eyebrow, split lip. Well, you've seen the picture. He has very bruised kidneys, passing blood from them, bruises everywhere else. He may have a few scars, but everything else should heal. His phone was stolen. Hard to say whether he was targeted, but the severity indicated maybe he was. What's he doing in Perth?'

'We simply don't know. He told us when he first started going over there that it was for Aunt Linda. Maybe she knows. I gave you her number ages ago ...'

'It probably doesn't matter much. The police have him, they'll get his prints. We'll know one way or the other. His assault is their problem to solve. If his activity over there had anything to do with our case over here, it will come out soon enough.'

'What if some reporter turns up on the doorstep?'

'Same as if one phones: "No comment" and send them on their way. If they don't go, tell them you're calling us. I'll come straight out if you need me.'

'Thanks, Ben. Bye.' Susannah turned to Darren and relayed the gist of the call. 'Do you think I should call Aunt Linda?'

'Couldn't hurt. I had a short call from her while you and Silvio were at the coast, offering condolences and help. I never thought to ask her why Dad was over there all the time. Do you think he and Mum were splitting up?'

'God, how would I know! We were *all* keeping secrets from each other!' She sighed, 'Dar, we *have* to rethink the way we do things, you and me. No more secrets. It's starting to look as if our family will only be you and me in the future. We must learn to confide and trust in each other. It's the only way we can stay close, and I *want* to stay close. You're my brother and I've ignored you for too long.'

Darren stepped over and gave his sister a warm hug. 'Yeah, no more secrets. We'll be right, Sis, if we stick to that.'

Ben sat at his desk, comparing two photographs. One was a composite picture of the prints lifted off the poison vials, the other was the set of Gordon's prints sent over from Western Australia. He felt depressed. Despite the fact both Susannah's and Darren's actions had slowed the investigation, he had developed a liking for them both. He recognised that their mother's murder had forced them both to mature, and they were more likeable because of it. He wished he didn't have to add to their troubles, but the two photographs matched in every way. He was reluctant to take the next step of requesting Gordon be extradited back to New South Wales. He procrastinated by calling Kaylee.

'When do the light duties start?'

'Better be soon, I'm bored rigid.'

Ben sighed. 'Make the most of the peace and quiet. The prints on the vials match Gordon's.'

'Wow! Great work. Poor Susannah and Darren,' she paused. 'Well, why are you wasting time talking to me? Have you requested extradition? We need Gordon back here immediately.'

'I know,' he said gloomily. 'I think it's "closure syndrome". You know, where the rush for suspects, clues, answers and so on, is over. And you're left feeling hollow and let down.'

'Is that what you call it?' Kaylee responded tartly. 'Well, you just get off your butt, stop feeling sorry for yourself and start on the next stage. We need Gordon here. We need to work on a water-tight case. There's plenty still to do, and I'm not there to take charge. Stop wallowing in your so-called "closure syndrome" and get to work. "Closure syndrome" I've never heard such rubbish! Get to work, and that's an order, even though I'm on sick leave!'

Ben heard the smile in her voice, but it was enough to motivate him, and he obediently followed her order.

Alone on a rugged hill high above his family home, Ali Hadji cried out his desolation and grief. In one day, he had lost the two women he loved absolutely. One woman, his wonderful mother, had given him the most stable childhood. Kind, funny, comforting, wise, she had helped him navigate through all his boyhood tribulations. She saw that he was getting in with a bad crowd of street fighters who would lead him into a life of trouble and shame. Her encouragement had seen him take his courage in both hands and travel to Australia to work. The other woman, Mrs Hathaway, culturally a hundred miles removed from his mother, strong, determined, volatile, intelligent. He had fallen passionately in love with her almost as soon as he met her. He adored the way her eyes crinkled when she was happy. Even when she was rapping out contradictory orders, he felt he could listen to her voice forever. His love was even stronger because it was his secret. *Who could have done this terrible thing to her?* Under his grief, he felt a deep rage begin to burn. He knew he could only ever worship her in his secret soul, but she was his and she was precious. *Whoever took her away from me so callously must be made to pay. A beautiful, vibrant, larger-than-life woman gone. Someone will have to suffer for her death.*

Gradually his turmoil subsided. He wiped away his tears and began to think rationally. He could do nothing here to avenge her death. He must return to Divine Hayfields and his job. Somehow, he must see that justice was meted out for the death of such a gloriously vivid woman. He walked down the hill and gently broke the news to his father and brothers that he would soon be going back to Australia.

'Mr Hathaway, you are not to attempt to leave. We will be putting a police guard on your door. We will advise New South Wales police that we have located you and we will wait for their advice.'

The two policemen left the room.

Gordon's whole body slumped. He suddenly seemed smaller. *Where is Antonia? Probably gone for good.* He'd lost his chance to climb up Perth's social strata on her coat tails. *How much more can go wrong?* He'd lost out on inheriting the stud. He'd lost his syndicate and his income. He'd been bashed awfully. Now, finally, the police had fixed on him for Felicity's murder. All his carefully laid plans were crumbling to dust. No money, no easy transition to Perth, no affluent woman to support him.

Miserably, he went over his mistakes. He realised now he should have made sure he knew how Felicity had bequeathed her assets. *How the hell could I have known about that snake, Mac?* He should have listened to the tiny voice that warned him the syndicate was a bad idea. The money he'd made on it was small comfort. He gloomily guessed it was probably gone too. His bank account was most likely cleaned out, since all his details had been in his phone. *Why was I so greedy and impatient?*

True to his nature, he began to blame everyone but himself and his lack of forethought for his troubles. It was

Felicity's fault for being so difficult. It was Linda's fault for spending her inheritance so foolishly. Antonia must have set out to trap him. *Who ese would have set me up for that vicious belting? Where are Darren and Susannah when I need them?* He conveniently ignored the fact he had walked out without giving any thought to them, hadn't even remembered he had no idea where Susannah was, had ignored all their calls. His mind was a swirling mass of despair. *Where is my life going from here?* He groaned under the weight of anguish and in genuine pain and discomfort. His kidneys hurt dreadfully, and it was very disquieting to see all the blood when he had to relieve himself. The doctor had said it was severe bruising and would heal given time. He wretchedly assumed all his physical wounds would heal eventually but as for everything else, *what a disaster! What a thorough botch I've made of everything.*

CHAPTER TWENTY-NINE

Spring had almost turned into summer. Foals frisked in the grassy paddocks while their glossy mothers grazed. Work was progressing smoothly at Divine Hayfields with the yearlings responding well to training and preparation for the forthcoming sales. On the surface life was returning to normal.

Mac still lived in Wheeler, travelling daily to the farm. He confidence with decision-making had grown, helped along by Jarred's unhesitating support. There were enough hands now to allow Mac and Jarred to have regular, extended planning discussions without fear that tasks would be neglected. They found they worked well together. The staff seemed more settled without Felicity's constant changes and Gordon's overbearing manner. Ali was welcomed back and was making daily progress with his leggy energetic charges. If he seemed sometimes quiet and abstracted, the lads sympathetically put it down to grief for his mother.

Darren moved all his office operations away from the main house to Jarred's office in the feed shed. He moved all his personal effects into the room he and Kevin shared in the cottage. Danny took over Hamish's cottage room.

Susannah arranged to rent Mr Thompson's house where she and Silvio now lived. Gisella was at first horrified to think that Silvio was "living in sin" but as usual her romantic nature soon took over from her scruples, and she spent many a happy hour in pleasant reveries about future weddings and christenings.

Gordon had been returned from Western Australia under police escort. Kaylee was bitterly disappointed not to be one of the escorting police because she was still on light duties. Ben couldn't resist teasing her that he had enjoyed his trip to Perth, even though, in reality it was simply a flight over and back with no time for pleasure.

After long and careful questioning, Gordon finally admitted to adding poison to Felicity's syringes. He was formally charged with her murder and was awaiting trial. His injuries healed well except for the kidney. Eventually, scans revealed an aneurysm which was the result of his beating. This was being regularly monitored by doctors. He used the ongoing medical needs as cause for applying for bail. Even though he had travelled to Western Australia when he'd been specifically requested by police to stay at the stud during their investigation, his application for bail was granted. He was forced to surrender his passport and drivers' licence, to live at Divine Hayfields homestead and obey a strict curfew. Because of his threatening manner towards Mac, a further requirement was that he not associate with Mac. This suited him just fine because he harboured a bitter resentment towards Mac.

Gordon spent his time morosely reflecting on all the things that had gone wrong for him. He could not accept that his troubles were all his own fault. He could only see all that he had lost. Being confined to the homestead served to remind him every day of how much his actions had cost him. He grew sullen and taciturn, taking no pleasure in any of the thriving farm life around him. He was curt to Darren and Susannah when they visited him with the result that their visits grew further and further apart. They were happier to immerse themselves in their new relationships than remind themselves of their ongoing sorrow for their mother and grief over their father's disastrous actions.

A little hiccup arose when Dell Sullivan refused to work "with that murderer in the house", so Mac hired a lass from Muswellbrook whose need for money overrode her principles about who was in the house she cleaned. Mrs Sullivan grandly informed Mac she would still be happy to carry out her duties in the lads' cottage. She suggested that rather than take a cut in wages, she could extend her duties to include cooking and shopping for the lads. This change was agreed to and welcomed by the lads, leading to an even more harmonious staff.

On the surface, life did indeed appear to be returning to normal. Underneath the surface, Gordon allowed his sullenness and feelings of ill-use to fester and grow, becoming more bitter and withdrawn each day.

Ali Hadji was comprehensively brought up-to-date on all the events that had taken place while he had been away. Gordon's arrest and bail conditions were common knowledge, but his health problems were not. Ali finally had a focus for his vengeful anger over the death of his darling Felicity. Every day he thought of ways to even the score for her with Gordon and everyday memories of his mother reminded him of the terrible and shameful consequences for himself and his family if he committed a crime. His hot anger burned while he tried to come up with a legal way to punish Gordon.

A couple of days before the yearling sales were due to be held, everyone was working extremely hard to finish preparations for the sale. Because the sale was to be held at the stud, carparking had to be cordoned off, refreshments had to be organised, the parade ring needed seating erected around it. Many jobs and not much time. Everyone was focused on their allotted task, concentrating on getting the job done.

Bored and morose, Gordon stepped off the veranda and strolled down to the big stable barn.

Ali Hadji finished cooling off a colt he'd been working with and walked it back into the big stable building. He took a few minutes while he secured the short lead to the ring and left, closing the stall door behind him. He almost collided with Gordon.

'Watch where you're going, you stinking camel jockey,' Gordon growled roughly. All Ali's fiercely bottled-up rage boiled to the surface. His street fighting instincts kicked in. With lightning speed, he closed his fists and punched Gordon, a quick one, two, in the kidney. The dormant aneurysm ruptured. Gordon gasped and dropped to his knees, bleeding internally. Ali left the stables without a backward glance.

Gordon felt the pain through a light-headed haze. He fell forward and breathed a few shallow breaths as he bled to death almost precisely where Felicity had died.

Kevin and Jarred walked into the barn, discussing last-minute chores before the sale. In the cool dim light, their eyes were drawn to something that looked like a large, crumpled chaff bag on the ground.

www.ingramcontent.com/pod-product-compliance
Lightning Source LLC
Chambersburg PA
CBHW032051020426
42335CB00011B/285